Leader As Coach

Strategies For Coaching and Developing Others

David B. Peterson, Ph.D. & Mary Dee Hicks, Ph.D.

A companion volume to
**Development First:
Strategies for Self-Development**
by David B. Peterson & Mary Dee Hicks

Personnel Decisions International
2000 Plaza VII Tower
45 South Seventh Street
Minneapolis, Minnesota 55402-1608
USA
612.339.0927

*We gratefully acknowledge the following
for their support and assistance in producing this book:*

Don Birkeland, Amy Carroll Collins, Brian Davis, Tom Eckstein,
Michael Frisch, Susan Gebelein, Keith Halperin, Ken Hedberg,
Dave Heine, Lowell Hellervik, Barb Iacarella, Susan James,
Teresa Jensen, Cindy Marsh, Lou Quast, Pete Ramstad,
Steven Snyder, Gwen Stucker, Dale Thompson, Jim Warner,
and Värde Partners

---

*We also appreciate those who reviewed earlier versions of this book
and provided valuable suggestions and insights:*

Tony Chapman, Fran Duncan, Joanne Ehren Dahlquist, Janet Dunn,
Marv Dunnette, Dennis Folz, Toni Graham, Fiona Grant,
Joy Hazucha, Martha Hill, Brad Maihack, Susan Mundale,
Bob Muschewske, Bob Myers, Sally Neverman, Donna Seefried, Elaine Sloan,
Jan Stambaugh, Karen Stellon, Marcia Sytsma, and Seymour Uranowitz

---

*Finally, we acknowledge the significant debt we owe to our clients,
who helped us craft and test these ideas.*

Design: The Kuester Group
Illustrator: Mary Grand Pré
Editorial Services: Mundale Communications, Gwen Stucker

Copyright 1996 by Personnel Decisions International Corporation

All rights reserved. No part of this material may be reproduced by
any means without permission in writing from the publisher.

Printed in the United States of America.

ISBN 0-938529-14-5

CONTENTS

Forge a Partnership: Build trust and understanding so people want to work with you.
Strategy 1, Page 27

Inspire Commitment: Build insight and motivation so people focus their energy on goals that matter.
Strategy 2, Page 53

Grow Skills: Build new competencies to ensure people know how to do what is required.
Strategy 3, Page 79

Promote Persistence: Build stamina and discipline to make sure learning lasts on the job.
Strategy 4, Page 95

Shape the Environment: Build organizational support to reward learning and remove barriers.
Strategy 5, Page 113

Coaching and development is not optional

We wrote this book to help you and your organization become more competitive by boosting your capacity to foster growth in others.

For years we have made it our business to help people develop and become more effective at work. We know how hard change can be. We also know how rewarding it is to help people do things they never thought possible. We want to share our techniques with you so that you can help people do their jobs better now and in the future. And so you, too, can experience the rewards of playing a critical part in their development.

We chose the "leader as coach" metaphor to broaden your vision of yourself as a leader. Like a sports coach who builds a competitive team, you must ensure that your players are capable and versatile. But where do you start? What's the best way to coach when every circumstance is different? And how can you find time to coach when you are already consumed with other responsibilities?

This book answers these questions with suggestions that address the escalating time pressures, constant change, and heightened complexity most leaders face. We have tried to make coaching manageable by distilling it into five powerful and practical strategies. But manageable does not mean simple, because the real world is not simple. People in the real world do not respond well to one-size-fits-all formulas. Our goal is to approach the complex challenge of development with sufficient practicality that you can actually make a difference.

We hope these ideas will help you to lead your people and your organization to greater success.

David B. Peterson & Mary Dee Hicks

> **The purpose of leadership is to create more leaders, not more followers.**

Coaching and Development: Your Competitive Edge

An organization's R&D – research and development – sharpens technical excellence and sustains competitive advantage. Similarly, an organization's C&D – coaching and development – sharpens and sustains the competitive advantage of human capital. Both R&D and C&D are integral to leveraging an organization's strategies and core competencies. Neglect of either type of development ultimately leads to mediocrity or failure.

"Our people are our most important asset" is not a trite slogan; it is a fundamental truth. People make your organization, and people who are world-class learners make your organization great. Year after year, the organizations that make the greatest innovations do so because they consistently invest in R&D. Only by also investing in coaching will you and your organization be able to develop the people who serve your customers, create your products, and manage your systems.[1]

As a leader on the front line of C&D, you can help translate the rhetoric of "people are our most important asset" into real investment in people's growth.

Capsule Preview

– *Why coaching and development?*

– *What is your personal payback?*

– *What is coaching?*

– *The secret of the 5% solution.*

– *Where do you invest your energy?*

– *What should you know about self-development?*

Why coaching and development?

> "The difference between transformation by accident and transformation by a system is like the difference between lightning and a lamp. Both give illumination, but one is dangerous and unreliable, while the other is relatively safe, directed, available."[2]

Like the effects from a bolt of lightning, development left to chance is unreliable. Purposeful C&D directs energy where you want it and powers systematic improvement in the competencies your organization needs.

For focused development to become a reality, leaders need to translate good intentions into action. Yet, according to a recent survey, many leaders admit that coaching is frequently a low priority in their organizations.[3]

- Managers around here don't take the time for coaching.
- Coaching gets put on the back burner.
- There is too much emphasis on results to spend much time on development.
- We give lots of lip service to coaching, but no real commitment.

To close this breach, C&D requires an infusion of leadership and commitment throughout your organization. Coaching cannot be limited to human resources or training departments, external vendors, or even to the occasional leader with a real knack for helping people grow. The following realities make C&D an imperative for every leader in your organization:

> The ability to learn faster than your competitors may be the only sustainable competitive advantage.
>
> *Arie De Geus*

Reality #1: Change is inevitable. Even the most successful organizations cannot rest on their laurels. They must continually remake themselves or risk falling from glory. IBM was *Fortune* magazine's most admired corporation for four years before plummeting into the bottom half of the ratings. After Merck claimed the leader's position on the list for seven years running, it rapidly lost its luster and fell from the top ten. Because today's excellence is no guarantee for tomorrow's success, leaders who bask in complacency are due for a rude awakening.

Reality #2: People must learn and adapt quickly. Your people's skills will become obsolete – in the same way technologies become outdated – if you rely solely on today's capabilities to lead your organization into the future. You cannot just hire talented people, teach them to do their jobs, and then leave them alone. To cope with the inevitability of changing work demands, you need a work force that can learn new skills and adapt quickly.

One way or another, most people figure out how to do their jobs. But development by default is too passive to achieve the standards of excellence and versatility that you must meet. Because the world refuses to wait for those who say "slow down while I gain more experience," organizations are looking for better and faster ways to achieve breakthrough performance with their people. Experience and time alone are slow and inefficient teachers. You need to jump-start learning and make sure it runs full speed in the right direction.

Reality #3: Employees want to grow. Lifelong employment in the same job is becoming a career path found only in history books. Some experts estimate that the career of the average college graduate today will include at least eight jobs in four different industries. Many job changes will be voluntary, because of the growing desire to find personal growth and satisfaction in work. People who feel underutilized will leave. Unfortunately for you, the people who depart for greener pastures could be the very ones you want to keep. To prevent talented, motivated people from being recruited by a competitor with better opportunities, you need to invest in their continuous growth and satisfaction.

Reality #4: People are the real source of competitive advantage. Versatile people – those who learn better and faster than your competition – sustain your edge in the marketplace. Because your people are your most important assets, coaching is your investment vehicle for long-term payback. With new development, people become:

- ***Competent:*** Possessing the skills to fulfill the requirements of their current and emerging jobs.
- ***Aligned:*** Sharing a sense of purpose and common values that motivate them to work constructively and consistently toward organizational objectives.
- ***Self-directed:*** Demonstrating personal responsibility, leadership initiative, and sound independent judgment in their work.
- ***Adaptable:*** Having the ability and motivation to continuously learn and adapt as their roles and organizational needs change.

> THE GREAT LEADERS OF TOMORROW WILL BE THE ONES WHO UNDERSTAND HOW TO GET EVERYONE TO PARTICIPATE.
>
> *Sara Little Turnbull*

What is your personal payback?

Despite the benefits to your organization, you are unlikely to sustain the discipline of coaching if you do not see what is in it for you. Beyond the personal satisfaction and pride you might feel from helping others grow, consider how you benefit from coaching others:

You build a stronger team. Highly capable people produce better results, and you bask in the glow of their success. Well-coached people are focused, adaptable, and resilient; hence they are less likely to be caught flatfooted by change. When they are growing, they deliver better results for you through their dedication, excitement, and productivity.

You become a magnet for talent. Topnotch talent flocks toward growth opportunities. You will lure the best and brightest people if you cultivate a reputation as a leader who helps people learn and grow. Moreover, growth and opportunity increasingly differentiate the organizations that can recruit top talent from those that cannot.

You sustain a network of support. Successful coaches often create career opportunities that lead people to new challenges. How could this outflow of talent have long-term benefits for you? As people move on, the organization will be seeded with people who appreciate your support. As your allies, they will be predisposed to help you in their new positions. They will also be able to promote the shared vision you developed when you worked together.

> People who are coaches will be the norm. Other people won't get promoted.
>
> *Jack Welch*

What is coaching?

Coaching is the process of equipping people with the tools, knowledge, and opportunities they need to develop themselves and become more effective.

Coaches equip people to develop themselves.

Coaches don't develop people – they equip people to develop themselves. Rarely will you have the time to involve yourself with every aspect of someone's development. And rarely will you possess all of the information, skills, and wisdom that someone might need to ensure their development. Fortunately, there is no need to be perfect to be an effective coach. Instead, view your role as a catalyst for development.

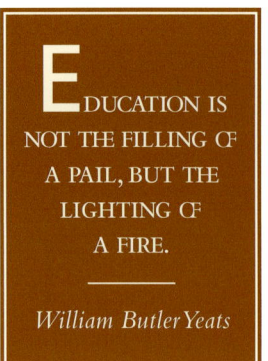

Education is not the filling of a pail, but the lighting of a fire.

William Butler Yeats

Coaching is a continuous process, not an occasional conversation – "Let's sit down and have a coaching session" – or a single event – "It's time for you to take the Advanced Leadership class." You might compare yourself to an orchestra conductor, so that sometimes you work one-on-one with a player, other times you direct them from afar, and on some occasions you cut people loose so they can develop in areas completely outside your scope. You guide them to learn and practice regularly, you help channel their passion to learn into the best opportunities, and you harmonize their playing with the other members of the organization.

THREE COACHING FRONTIERS.

Because each development challenge is unique, there are no cookbook formulas or automatic prescriptions. But there are three frontiers that are vital to multiplying your hands and sustaining the development quest over the long haul. As you read this book, look for ideas you can use on each frontier. If you have large numbers of people to coach or you coach people from afar, pay particular attention to the last two frontiers.

Working one-on-one. Part of coaching is direct and personal. Offer first-hand feedback, challenge people to take appropriate risks, and encourage them when they face setbacks and barriers.

Guiding people to learn for themselves. Because you are not always present when people encounter an opportunity to learn something new, you must arm them as crusaders on behalf of their own development. Teach them how to extract the right lessons from their experiences, how to find other people who can assist them, and how to obtain their own feedback and information.

Orchestrating resources and learning opportunities. You not only equip people to learn, but you intervene with others on their behalf as well. Foster an environment that supports intelligent risk-taking, find people who can teach or mentor them, break down barriers that inhibit continuous learning, and open doors to new experiences that they could not access without your help.

> GIVE A MAN A FISH AND YOU FEED HIM FOR A DAY. TEACH A MAN TO FISH AND YOU FEED HIM FOR A LIFETIME.
>
> *Chinese Proverb*

Common misperceptions about coaching

Coaching takes a lot of time. It is common to assume that coaches deliver hours and hours of private tutoring. While personal instruction is sometimes important, a coach's chief responsibility is to promote the development of others. Coaches leverage a variety of techniques, including orchestrating other resources that can offer teaching and tutoring.

Coaching is for fixing problem behaviors. If you pay attention only to problems, you will miss significant opportunities. The real goals of coaching are to cultivate people's capabilities and to tap their true potential. Rookies and all-stars alike benefit from coaching.

Coaching means giving feedback and advice. A "coaching session" for feedback and advice is only one vehicle for development. Coaches rely on many techniques to increase people's insight into themselves and to guide them to change.

Coaching is the same as mentoring. Mentors typically share insights and lessons from their personal storehouse of experiences and opportunities. Coaches paint development with a broader brush; they understand the process of learning and help create the conditions for it to occur.

Coaching is just a fad. Actually, leaders throughout history have coached their people to enhance their capabilities. Whether helping people adapt to change or getting new people up to speed, coaching is a perennially powerful leadership tool.

The secret of the 5% solution

By now you may be saying, "But my plate is already full. I can't handle one more obligation. I rarely see my people because I'm so busy and they are scattered all over the place. There's no way I can do all of this."

You face a dilemma: Simple solutions don't work for development, yet you don't have time for complex solutions. So you need a coaching process that attacks the true challenges of getting a variety of people to change and yet is still manageable in light of available time and resources. That process is the 5% solution.

Simple solutions don't work, but who has time for complex ones?

You can be effective and efficient if you focus 5% of your energy and attention on C&D. Working smarter – not working harder – helps you make the best investment of your time. The secret of efficient coaching is to know your priorities and then to create and seize coaching opportunities that arise in the course of your everyday work. If you are prepared, you can leverage a relatively small investment of your time into a walloping payback.

Where do you invest your energy?

1. Forge a Partnership
2. Inspire Commitment
3. Grow Skills
4. Promote Persistence
5. Shape the Environment

Once you commit 5% of your energy and attention, how do you spend it? In the areas where people's development is most likely to break down:
- People do not understand their development needs.
- People do not make development a priority.
- People do not know how to learn the skills they need.
- People do not believe you care about them or their development.
- People do not translate good intentions into real change on the job.
- People do not see organizational incentives for developing.

The coaching strategies. The following strategies target these common development barriers.

1. Forge a Partnership. Build trust and understanding so people want to work with you. With trust, people will be more willing to hear and act on what you have to say. With understanding, you will know what matters to each other.

2. Inspire Commitment. Build insight and motivation so people focus their energy on goals that matter. You cannot motivate people directly, but you can achieve commitment to development when people understand themselves and the personal payback from working toward organizational objectives.

3. Grow Skills. Build new competencies to ensure people know how to do what is required. When you know what the person needs to develop, your task is to help them find the best ways to acquire those new skills.

4. ***Promote Persistence.*** Build stamina and discipline to make sure learning lasts on the job. People require daily effort to change old habits and put new behaviors into action. You can help people persist until their new behaviors become natural.

5. ***Shape the Environment.*** Build organizational support to reward learning and remove barriers. Change is easier and the results last longer when the organization's values and rewards are aligned with coaching and development.

The rest of this book shows you how to use these five strategies. As you coach different people, you may find yourself starting with almost any strategy depending on which barrier needs to be addressed. Or, you might work several strategies simultaneously. Ultimately, for development to work, all must be in place.

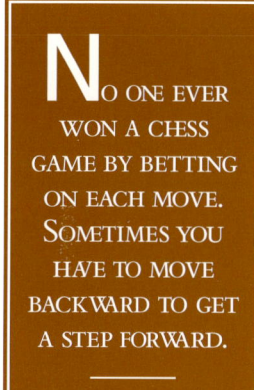

No one ever won a chess game by betting on each move. Sometimes you have to move backward to get a step forward.

Amar Bose

What should you know about how people develop themselves?

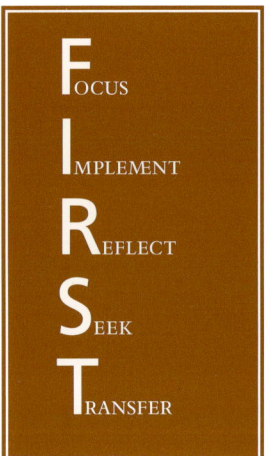

Because development is a partnership, you do not take full responsibility for C&D. The people you coach have a high stake in development as well, and they actually bear the bulk of the day-to-day work. Because coaching supports people's efforts to develop themselves, you need a good understanding of what self-development entails.

The self-development strategies. While self-development is described in more detail in the book, *Development FIRST: Strategies for Self-Development,* here is a brief summary to get you started:

- **Focus** *on priorities: Identify your critical issues and goals.* People start by focusing on development goals that matter both to them and to the organization. Then they create a plan for development that supports them along the way. Focusing on one or two goals helps people find the energy and resources to carry through on their development.

- **Implement** *something every day: Stretch your comfort zone.* Development goals and tactics need to be translated into daily action to make change a reality. Like a disciplined exercise program, people can identify concrete opportunities for growth and address the emotions and external challenges that threaten to drive them off course.

- **Reflect** *on what happens: Extract maximum learning from your experiences.* Without pausing to consolidate and assimilate learning experiences, the lessons can go to waste. People need to distill what worked well, what went awry, and what they plan to do differently the next time they try.

- **Seek** *feedback and support: Learn from others' ideas and perspectives.* With the ongoing ballast and support of coaches and other resources, people can sustain motivation and stay on course. They also gather relevant information about their progress so they know how they are doing.

- **Transfer** *to next steps: Adapt and plan for continued learning.* Periodically, people should step back from their plan for development and take stock of their progress. Is it time to revise their goals? What else can they do to solidify their learning or to keep moving forward? Then they can cycle back to the first self-development strategy, *Focus,* to maintain a cycle of continuous, life-long learning.

When you use the coaching strategies, you reinforce people's commitment to the FIRST strategies at the same time. You might also want to teach people this process directly and use it to diagnose where their development efforts are not succeeding.

Three development groups

The end of each *Leader As Coach* chapter provides practical tips for applying the coaching strategies. Your coaching approach generally falls into one of three broad categories, based on people's unique needs and situations.

1. Set the standard. The people in this category are not performing at the desired level and need to add new competencies to their repertoires. People in this group might be new in their roles or they might be veterans whose skills are below standard.
- *New job.* John was just promoted to a district sales manager job after five stellar years on the street making sales calls. He doesn't know the first thing about budget management or supervising others.
- *Stretch assignment.* Abigail, a solid technical manager, is leading a major cross-functional product development effort and is struggling to coordinate and influence the many players on her team.
- *Underperformance.* Although Victor has been a senior financial planner for two years and everyone loves working with him, he is still not meeting his revenue goals because of his inefficiency and lack of planning.

2. Set new direction. People in this group have to unlearn old behaviors and learn new skills. Typically, they are performing well today, but their skills will be obsolete or insufficient as priorities evolve and new challenges become a reality. Changes in work demands, organizational strategies, or competitive forces might precipitate the need for a new direction. Sometimes the emerging demand for change is subtle, because needs are being met and people have been succeeding. But alert leaders recognize that the status quo will quickly fall short in a changing environment.
- *New customer focus.* Kevin's department has become serious about delivering tailored solutions to customers. A veteran plant manager,

he needs to shed his "I'm the boss" style and develop new techniques for leading a more responsive work force.
- *Downsizing.* William has been the mainstay of the marketing department, but with a downsizing wave heading his way, he has to figure out how to meet his demands with a much smaller and less specialized staff to handle production, analysis, and follow-up duties.
- *Tougher competition.* While Marcia, the research manager, has perennially delivered aggressive product upgrades, agile new competitors with innovative products are threatening to soften the product foothold in some segments. Unless she can revitalize the department and quickly inspire breakthrough innovations, the strong sales trends will begin to reverse.
- *Turbulent growth.* Booming business is stretching current staff to their limits. How can Tony balance delivering on today's demands with the need to build new systems to handle the increased volume?

3. Set free. In this group, you help people soar toward their full potential. They need to stretch their limits and find fresh applications for their skills so they do not become stale or restless. You might not notice these development needs if people are content within their comfort zone and they are meeting organizational needs. Sometimes you need to stir people up and expose them to new possibilities to get maximum yield from their talents.
- *Rising star.* As an ambitious software programming whiz, Lydia quickly surpassed her boss's technical depth. If she is stretched and challenged as a leader, she has the potential to be the next R&D director.
- *Unrecognized talent.* Lee's creative flair has long added spice to the internal newsletter, but he has shied away from opportunities to test out his gift with the marketing and advertising group.
- *Turnover risk.* Janis has been content for years to be one of the best analysts on the audit team, but she is beginning to feel bored and is responding to calls from headhunters.

Personal action steps

As you develop yourself as a coach:

Make coaching personal. Since coaching is more art than science, this is not a book of prescriptions or a fix-it manual. The ideas and actions have to resonate for you and fit the complexion of your work relationships and personality. Find your own coaching style by selecting and adapting the pieces that suit you best.

Reflect. Take a minute to reflect on what you have learned so far. How will these lessons change your approach to coaching?

Start your own learning log. Devise a practical way to record your most important coaching insights and priorities. For example, how do you plan to devote 5% of your attention to C&D? How will you drive and track your own development as a coach? How can you get help from your coach?

Pick one person to coach now. Select one person you want to coach. As you read further, think about how you can use the ideas and suggestions with this person. Refer to the framework of the three common development categories in the preceding section to think through their unique needs. At the end of each remaining chapter, you will be guided in applying the coaching strategies with this person.

Begin a plan for coaching the person you have chosen.
Use a format that you are comfortable with, but make sure your plan helps you:
- Define your objectives for the person's development.
- Specify how you will accomplish your objectives. Decide which things make the most sense to orchestrate through others, pursue directly with the person, or teach them to do for themselves.
- Periodically take stock of how well things are working.

1. Forge a Partnership

Build trust and understanding so people want to work with you.

Leader As Coach

Jump-start

Forging a partnership is most important when:

- *The person does not know much about you.*
- *You don't know what motivates the person or what they really care about.*
- *You have not worked as the person's coach before.*
- *The person is skeptical or cynical about the organization's leadership.*
- *You are not sure what they think of you, your motives, and your competence.*
- *The person risks losing something they value because of organizational changes.*
- *You have had significant conflicts with the person.*
- *The person complains about being kept in the dark on important issues.*
- *You don't trust the person's candor or intentions.*

To strengthen your partnership:

- *Listen carefully to understand the person's interests, opinions, and concerns.*
- *Pay attention to what excites the person and what choices they make.*
- *Discuss junctures where trust might have broken down in the past.*
- *Clarify your expectations for each other.*
- *Provide candid yet tactful feedback.*
- *Show the person how you are trying to take their best interests into account.*
- *Respect the person's limits and preferences.*
- *Follow up with the person to demonstrate that you have lived up to your commitments.*
- *Have a coach yourself.*

Strategy 1
FORGE A PARTNERSHIP

Within a blast furnace, crude iron and chromium meld into stainless steel. Left cool and separate, the raw materials remain dark and brittle; together they become gleaming and resilient. Like a vessel for developmental combustion, your coaching partnership creates the conditions to meld people's raw materials into new talents and capabilities. Without the energy and crucible of a partnership, the elements are inert or underdeveloped. Within a partnership, something new is forged from the elements, something stronger and more versatile than either element alone.

When you address the fundamentals of your relationship, you create a foundation for coaching and set the conditions for people to change. The need for this foundation was repeatedly reinforced in a recent series of interviews asking managers about the things they valued most from being coached. The top two elements? Candid dialog and a relationship with a caring, supportive coach. As one manager claimed, "Without trust, there is no coaching."[4]

> **CAPSULE PREVIEW**
>
> – *Tune in to the person's view of the world.*
>
> – *Build a bond of trust.*
>
> – *Test your trust level.*
>
> – *Restore trust.*
>
> – *Respect ethical boundaries.*

Why is a strong partnership so critical?

Mutual understanding. With trust, you are willing to open up to each other and talk about what really matters. Coaching has to be directed at what people care about or it becomes an empty exercise.

People are more willing to follow your lead. When people believe that you understand and care about them, they are more likely to get hooked on working with you on their development.

People are more willing to take risks. Meaningful development entails working at the edge of people's comfort zone. People will take more risks when they trust your judgment and intentions.

Tune in to the Person's View of the World

You forge a partnership when people believe you understand what's important to them. No partnership can thrive at arm's length. People will be slow to get on board if your entreaties to "just trust me" are not clearly based on your genuine interest in what they value and how they view the world.

Set your mind on exploring, not fixing. The first step is to temporarily let go of your desire to help, motivate, or change people, and instead simply try to understand them. Assume that no two people are alike in their values, goals, motives, and experiences. Like a detective solving a mystery, you need to uncover clues about the unique ways in which each individual views the world.

Look for the right evidence. Three types of evidence about people's world views are particularly relevant to your development partnership:

1. What excites them?
- Where do you see their greatest energy and enthusiasm?
- What themes do they talk about most frequently?
- What activities and assignments do they seek or volunteer for?

If you want people to work harder, be smarter, and jump higher, then you have to know what will get them moving. When you know their answer to "Why should I try?," you can wrap your strategy around the things that are relevant and motivating to them.

2. How do they view themselves?
- How do they appraise their skills and abilities?
- Which skills do they believe they have and which do they covet?
- Are they wracked with self-doubt or are they basking in self-content?

Their self-assessed competence guides you in providing feedback and devising your coaching strategy. Your tactics with someone who has an inflated self-evaluation will differ from your approach with someone who significantly undervalues their abilities. Self-appraisal also provides critical information about which development objectives people will choose to pursue.

3. **What do they believe about their ability to develop?**
- Are they confident they can change?
- Are they willing to take risks to change?
- Do they think their development will make a difference?

People who believe their capabilities are predetermined or constrained by outside forces need to learn to influence their own developmental destiny. Those who fear failure need to be emboldened.

Listen carefully. The best way to discover another person's world view is to listen to them. If you do not already practice the fundamentals of listening – paraphrasing and asking open questions – get training and develop these skills now. The best courses teach listening techniques through practice and give you guidance in applying the skills back on the job. Books on the subject can further round out your skills and help you build a mindset conducive to open listening.

> Listening is a magnetic and creative force. The friends who listen to us are the ones we move toward.
>
> *Karl Menninger*

Whatever techniques you use, the litmus test of effective listening is whether other people feel understood, not whether you believe you understand. Because one of the most common errors in making self-evaluations is the belief that we are much better listeners than others perceive us to be, take these steps to make sure your listening is up to par:
- At the end of each coaching encounter, summarize these critical dimensions of the person's perspective: their thoughts, intentions, and feelings. Ask them to verify or correct your understanding.
- Get feedback on your listening. Ask people if they feel you understand them and if you give them sufficient opportunity to express what they think is important.
- You cannot understand someone through a sound bite of information or even through a single heart-to-heart talk. Make a commitment to listen to them throughout their development journey. You have two eyes, two ears, and one mouth. Use them proportionately.

Tune in to high-fidelity sources. While you can glean some insights with relatively little effort, you should also turn your antennae toward the situations that are often packed with clues about what is important to people. In each circumstance, try to understand and verify the causes of people's actions and feelings.

New challenges heighten people's energy and apprehension. They are ripe with clues about people's motives and self-assessment.
- "Why are you so excited to work with Randy on this project?"
- "This is a big opportunity. How are you feeling about your ability to handle it right now?"

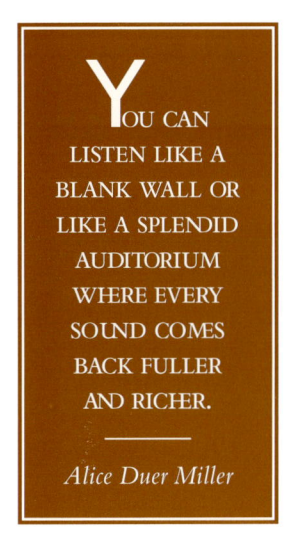

> YOU CAN LISTEN LIKE A BLANK WALL OR LIKE A SPLENDID AUDITORIUM WHERE EVERY SOUND COMES BACK FULLER AND RICHER.
>
> *Alice Duer Miller*

Demonstrations of strong emotions nearly explode with potential information about what people value, fear, and reject.
- "You are really balking at the prospect of working on the task force. Help me understand why."
- "I know you're upset because the presentation didn't go as well as you would like. Tell me what you're thinking about what happened."

Unexpected behavior suggests that some aspect of people's world view is yet to be uncovered. You have an opportunity to probe each time they veer in an unexpected direction and you find yourself wondering: "Why in the world would they want to do that?"
- "I thought you were enthusiastic about cultivating your technical skills, but now you are talking about the management opening over in production. Help me understand why."

BUILD A BOND OF TRUST

If you are like most people, you see yourself as basically trustworthy and you may be tempted to skip this section. But do not take trust for granted. No matter how trustworthy you are as a person, the following conditions make it hard for others to trust anyone:
- Significant surprises, unpredictability, and stress in the environment.
- Lack of a sense of safety and security.
- Fear of losing something important.
- Uncertainty about other people's intentions.

> THE LAMB AND THE LION SHALL LIE DOWN TOGETHER, BUT THE LAMB WILL NOT BE VERY SLEEPY.
>
> *Woody Allen*

Times of change are particularly rife with these conditions, resulting in the dilemma that people often do not trust their leaders precisely when coaching might be most helpful. This manager's experience highlights all four challenges to trust:

We just went through restructuring. The fear level was way up. Even though I lived through a takeover several years ago, I never saw this level of tension. Along the way, everyone tended to avoid talking about what was going on. Management was protecting people and not telling us everything. We didn't manage the tension. We didn't really use the opportunity to understand each other because people were protecting their turf. We're finally beginning to settle down now, but now we're left with bitterness along with the relief.

Perhaps the chief difficulty of trust arises when people fail to recognize its absence. When you don't verify trust, you might believe that people have been open with you when in fact they provided only part of the story. Or, you might assume that they trust your candor and intentions, when in fact they don't.

Do not take trust for granted.

If people seem to be dragging their feet, coaches often assume that they are not motivated to change. Instead of jumping to this conclusion, consider the possibility that trust, not motivation, is the missing element. When you see the following, be alert to the possibility that trust might be shaky:
• Suspicion and accusations of hidden agendas.
• Lip service and benign neglect of plans or agreed-upon actions.
• Defensiveness and blaming others when problems arise.
• Territoriality and protection of self-interest to the detriment of common interests.

Avoid the sins of omission. Odds are you will not deliberately set out to lie, cheat, or deceive. But even well-intentioned leaders fall into trust traps because of things they fail to do.

To keep trust strong, audit your trust level on these fronts:
• Do people know what to expect from you?
• Do people believe you do what you say?
• Do people believe you pay attention to their interests?
• Do people believe you are competent to carry out what you say?

Trust Test 1: Do people know what to expect from you?

People value predictability in their world so they can anticipate changes, make decisions, and set plans. Yet leaders often keep people in the dark about where they are going or what they are planning. In the absence of good information, people draw their own conclusions. Guesswork is a shaky foundation for trust.

Test yourself. Test whether the person you are coaching knows what to expect from you:
- How often do I try to protect the person by keeping information and concerns to myself?
- How much do I keep special information to myself so I can feel in-the-know?
- How often do I make decisions without sharing how or why I arrived at my conclusion?
- How active is the grapevine or rumor mill among the people I work with? How often is it accurate?
- To what extent am I concerned that the person can't be trusted to handle sensitive information responsibly?
- How willing am I to tell the person what I really think about their development needs?

Based on your answers, evaluate how likely it is that people do not know what to expect from you. Then consider strengthening trust with the following:

Offer status reports and forecasts. To avoid unnecessary guesswork, tell people what you do and don't know, as well as what you can and cannot tell them.
- "I haven't heard anything about the next downsizing. As soon as I know something that I can share with you I will pass it on."
- "I know we won't fill that position until next year."
- "Plans for the new contract are in the works, but I can't give you any details yet."

Convey consistent principles. Even when decisions cannot be predicted, you can cultivate certainty around the principles you will use to guide your decisions. Share your priorities. Let people know how you are trying to balance individual and organizational interests and the decision-making process you will use.

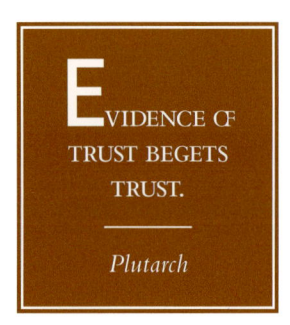

Give people plausible explanations for your actions. Sometimes your intentions are not readily apparent to others because you are taking multiple factors into account. Or, if the situation is obviously complex, people will often suspect simplistic motives. In the midst of major change, "I'm from corporate and I'm here to help you" gets laughed out of the room because everyone knows that more elaborate agendas are at work.

- Make sure your intentions and priorities match the complexity of the situation. "I'm trying to respond to the divisional need for greater productivity. At the same time, I'm trying to be supportive because I know everyone is stressed."
- Explain changes and apparent discrepancies in your actions. "I know that I haven't taken coaching seriously in the past. With your new responsibilities, I realize that I have to pay more attention to your development."

> **EVIDENCE OF TRUST BEGETS TRUST.**
>
> *Plutarch*

Balance candor with prudence. Common advice such as "Communicate, communicate, communicate" or "Just tell it like it is" betrays a simplistic understanding of the role of communication in a relationship. Complete disclosure of opinions, information, and confidences may erode trust and esteem just as quickly as secrets and hidden agendas.

To ensure that your communications balance usefulness, respect, and honesty, edit what you say by asking these questions:
- Does this information avoid breaches of confidence?
- How sensitive is it to the person's feelings and values?
- When is the best time and place to share it?
- Can the person use the information appropriately for making decisions and taking action?
- Will it help the person anticipate their future or see the world in a way that benefits them?
- If I have tough news, does the likely benefit of sharing it outweigh the potential harm? Is it motivated by genuine benevolence and a high likelihood of being helpful?
- Is it intended to help the person, not enhance my control or stature?

Trust Test 2: Do people believe you do what you say?

> It makes all the difference in the world whether you put truth in the first place or in the second place.
>
> *John Morley*

While the need to do what you say seems obvious, failure to do so is a common way for leaders to self-destruct on trust. Many people have observed leaders do things like:
- Say "I'll find out about that project over in the other division," and then not follow up with information on the project.
- Claim "We're launching a system-wide review process," then complete only partial implementation with no apparent commitment or further explanation.

Test yourself. Audit your consistency in living up to your word:
- How frequently does the person have to follow up with me on things I have agreed to do?
- How often do I drop the ball or let new priorities take precedence over previous commitments?
- How often do I try to solve an immediate problem by committing to things I probably can't do?

If your consistency in delivering on your word is uneven, focus on the following tactics:

Make realistic commitments. Trust is skewered when your expressions of support and promises of help are not backed with action. Sometimes you will not be able to do what you would like to do, so first you have to admit your limits to yourself. Then, communicate them to others.
- If you cannot promise an outcome, instead of simply admitting, "I can't make any promises," convey a realistic prediction: "I am going to lobby for the salary increases, but there is a 50-50 chance I'll get turned down."
- Apprise people of the process and parameters that you will follow: "I will be reviewing the recommendations with the group on Tuesday, and I don't expect a decision until next month."

Explain changes in your plans. Sometimes you need to adapt to changing situations. It is OK to change your plans, but let people know what changed. "I just got an urgent request and won't be able to get back to you next week."

Close the loop. Sometimes you may do what you promised, but people never find out. This is a particularly insidious trust-trap; you followed through, yet people's doubts are brewing. Avoid this trap by closing the loop promptly and deliberately.

Trust Test 3: Do people believe you pay attention to their interests?

No one can realistically expect you always to protect their interests. You are juggling obligations and constituents like an octopus and you cannot always favor one over the others. But despite your multiple loyalties, people need to believe that you are on their side.

Test yourself. Evaluate how well you show people you are representing their interests:
- How often do I try to convince someone that their concerns are less important than other priorities? "Don't worry about whether you will head the project team, we have to fix this problem first."
- How often do I lobby for rewards and opportunities for the person without their knowledge or their expectation that I do so?
- How often does the person see me compromising the interests of others, even if they might benefit? "I know José is expecting to go, but I'm inviting you on this customer visit instead."
- How often have they seen me share information about others that might be perceived as a breach of confidence?

People's trust that you are on their side will be greater if you:

Provide evidence of a win/win strategy. If you promote certain interests at the expense of others, even the people who come out ahead will suspect your motives on the next round. Genuinely promote the best possible solution for all parties. Then let people know what you have done to be fair.

Protect the interests of those who aren't present. The temptation to bring people into your confidence by sharing insider information or criticizing others can be very compelling. The short-term gain is often a feeling of special trust with your confidant. But when you share confidences or criticisms with people, you ultimately erode their willingness to share their vulnerability, weaknesses, and concerns with you.

Show compassion. Implement decisions with sensitivity, especially decisions with negative consequences for them. "I know you're disappointed that you didn't get the job. I'll keep you in mind in the future. In the meantime, let's work on your development to make sure you are really ready."

Also, because development requires hard work and nudges people beyond their comfort zone, it is often charged with apprehension. Acknowledge people's vulnerability and queasiness without discounting, placating, or threatening their self-confidence. "I know it's hard for you to go in front of senior management with this presentation. But I wouldn't suggest it if I didn't think you would handle it just fine."

Verify understanding. People need to be convinced that you understand their desires, concerns, and needs before they can trust that you will accurately represent their interests. Don't assume that people know what you are trying to accomplish on their behalf. Use good listening skills to draw them out, and verify your understanding with paraphrases, "Your concern is..." or "What you really want is..."

Trust Test 4: Do people believe you are competent to carry out what you say?

Even if people trust that your heart is made of gold and your mission is to care for their well-being, they will balk if they don't believe you can do what you claim. You must demonstrate that you have the skills, judgment, and organizational influence to deliver on your promises.

Test yourself. Test whether your competence might be in question:
- How well established is my track record on this topic?
- How well does this person know my capabilities?
- Is the person more experienced than I am?
- Does the person know of noteworthy failures I have had recently?
- How often does the person challenge or contradict my advice or decisions?

Here are some ways you can convince people they are in good hands with you:

Admit your limits. Leaders whose confidence exceeds their ability are often the most suspect. Your best intentions cannot compensate for perceived incompetence, and vacant assurances are no substitute for an honest admission of your limitations.

You have to know the bounds of your own capabilities before you can expect others to place trust in you. Coming to terms with what you can and cannot do may require a hefty dose of courage, but it is the prerequisite for honesty and genuineness in relating to others. Delineate what you can do for your coaching partner and when they will need to go elsewhere for help. Show that you know how to tap the expertise of others when you don't have the answers yourself.

Showcase what you know. Without being boastful, find opportunities to share relevant information with others about your experience, expertise, and other qualifications. Publicly work to stay current in your field and to develop your capabilities as a coach. Have the person talk with other people you have successfully coached.

Find opportunities to demonstrate that you know how to get things done in the organization. Share with others what you know about getting things done. Who has important information? Who needs to be in the loop? What are the ins and outs of getting authorizations?

Restore trust

Even with the best intentions, you will sometimes find that trust has broken down. You might step into a hornets' nest of old mistrust, make mistakes in your judgment and communications, or forget to follow through on a promise. When you need to restore trust, try the following:

Make the first move. To create the conditions for rebuilding trust, you must often play your cards first. You might need to reveal your agenda, be more daring with your opinions, and disclose more personally than you have before. When you do this, you reset the terms for your relationship, raise the standard for frank talk, and promote discussions of substantive issues. All of these induce others to trust in return.
- "The mood around here is pretty tense and it's making it difficult for me to help you. Given your past experiences with new managers, I can understand why you are skeptical about my intentions, but we aren't going to make much progress until we can get our concerns on the table."
- "I know we have had some pretty heated disagreements in the past. But now I want to work together with you on the strategic demands of your new job. Let's talk about what it will take for us to feel like we are in the same camp."

Admit your mistakes. People can forgive your mistakes, but they will fault you for pretending nothing is wrong. You can almost guarantee that your plans and actions will sometimes fail to live up to their billing, so take your knocks, clear the air, and learn from the mistakes together. Muster the honesty to admit to yourself that you were wrong and the courage to say "I'm sorry." You may even want to reflect back on your history with your partner, looking for junctures where your trust in each other might have been shaken. Your courage in exploring potentially uncomfortable and unflattering topics strengthens trust.

- "I really blew it when I didn't call you in on the contract negotiation. I knew you had a history with that customer, but things were moving so fast I didn't keep you in the loop. I'm sorry I cut you out of the action."
- "I know I pulled some strings to get some of your best people transferred to my project last year. In retrospect, that was pretty shortsighted."

Respect ethical boundaries

If you are an effective coach, you are a powerful force for change and wield a great deal of influence. As in all relationships of power, you must be fortified with high standards of personal ethics. You need a clear sense of your limits and the limits of the people you coach.

Protect people.
- ***Do no harm.*** Gauge how much you challenge others, what you expect from them, and how your plan for their development holds up against this standard: Does the benefit for the person clearly outweigh the risks they assume?
- ***Respect confidentiality.*** Few things can breach trust more fundamentally than crossing the perceived bounds of confidentiality. Take little for granted when deciding what you can say to whom about what. Clear your information with its source before you pass it on.
- ***Respect others' values.*** Don't expect people to want what you want or to care about the things that are important to you. Their fundamental values are unlikely to change. Admit that they might accept, with full awareness, the consequences of not changing.
- ***Respect people's limits.*** Unlike soft clay that can be pressed into infinite shapes, people evolve from a stable core. They can change in degree and bend in new directions, but they are unlikely to change in dramatic ways, at least not quickly. Respect their judgment about their own limits. Carefully evaluate how much change and what kind of change is fair to expect, especially if you are aware of changes or problems in other parts of their life or if they begin to appear distressed and confused.

- **Respect vulnerability.** In order for people to develop, they must trade the tried and true for the risk of failure, criticism, and embarrassment. They must seek and accept help even if they have been experts in the past, and they often must confront the parts of themselves that they like the least. They need to work very hard, often facing setbacks and snail-paced progress. You need to acknowledge that change is hard and be sensitive to their vulnerability in the process.

Work within your limits.
- **Steer clear of providing therapy.** Therapists, like coaches, help people change by showing compassion and honesty. But unlike coaches, therapists are trained to deal with significant emotional and behavioral challenges. Refer people elsewhere for professional help if you think you are in over your head.
- **Do not play the "white knight."** Your job is not to rescue people or to take personal responsibility for them. Maintain sufficient professional detachment so their success or failure does not become your success or failure. People often resent those who meddle or assume responsibility for their problems or careers. And you may be going too far if you feel like you are working harder on their development than they are.
- **Protect your boundaries.** If you are a trusted coach and confidant, people might impose on your time, push too far, or tell you secrets you don't want to know. Let people know when they have gone too far and you don't want to be involved. Sometimes you might lose objectivity or detect a conflict of interest. Because of the complexity of these issues, it is helpful to consult with others to keep your boundaries clear.

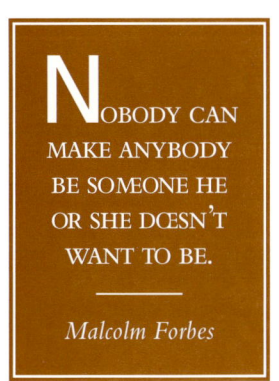

> **NOBODY CAN MAKE ANYBODY BE SOMEONE HE OR SHE DOESN'T WANT TO BE.**
>
> *Malcolm Forbes*

Tips to help you partner for trust and understanding

- Ask the people you coach for straight feedback on how well you understand their views.
- Stop and listen when people become emotional about important topics so you can learn more about what really matters to them.
- Schedule five minutes in your regular one-on-one meetings to learn about the person's interests and feelings about work.
- Express empathy for the challenges that the person is facing.
- Find out what people really think of you by using multi-rater feedback surveys or holding a heart-to-heart talk with a colleague who will tell it like it is.
- Explore how your decisions and actions are affected by your own values; then ask others how they see your values reflected in your actions.
- Make an appointment every few months to talk about your priorities and the direction of the organization. Invite and respond to any questions that people have.
- When visiting at remote sites, arrive early and schedule a breakfast or dinner with people.
- Use a variety of vehicles – E-mail, phone mail, printed bulletins, face-to-face meetings, teleconferences – to communicate regular updates and talk about your decisions and changes.
- Keep a running list of what is most important to your people. Review it every quarter.
- Establish an open forum where people can convey to you their concerns, opinions, and reactions.
- Ask people what barriers they see in establishing a positive working relationship with you.
- Take a class on active listening.
- Read the chapters on trust and understanding in Stephen Covey's *Seven Habits of Highly Effective People*.[5]

Personal action steps

Not much matters unless you put C&D into action right away and every day. You can get started even without a perfect understanding of the situation or a perfect plan of attack. With that bias for action in mind:

Master the basics. As you apply this strategy, make sure you have a solid foundation in:
- Listening skills.
- Insight into your own goals and values.
- Communicating your views clearly and directly.

How will you ensure a strong partnership with the person you are coaching?
- How did you do on the trust tests? What can you do to solidify the person's trust in you?
- How well do you understand what really matters to this person? What else do you need to learn about their view of the world?
- What potential barriers to coaching this person have you identified? What can you do to address the barriers?

What have you learned so far about yourself as a coach?
- What insights do you want to remember from this chapter? Enter them in your learning log.
- What one or two things would make the most difference in your coaching?

Where will you begin to take action?
- What ideas are you going to try first?
- What will you incorporate into your plans for coaching others?
- What else do you need for your own development?

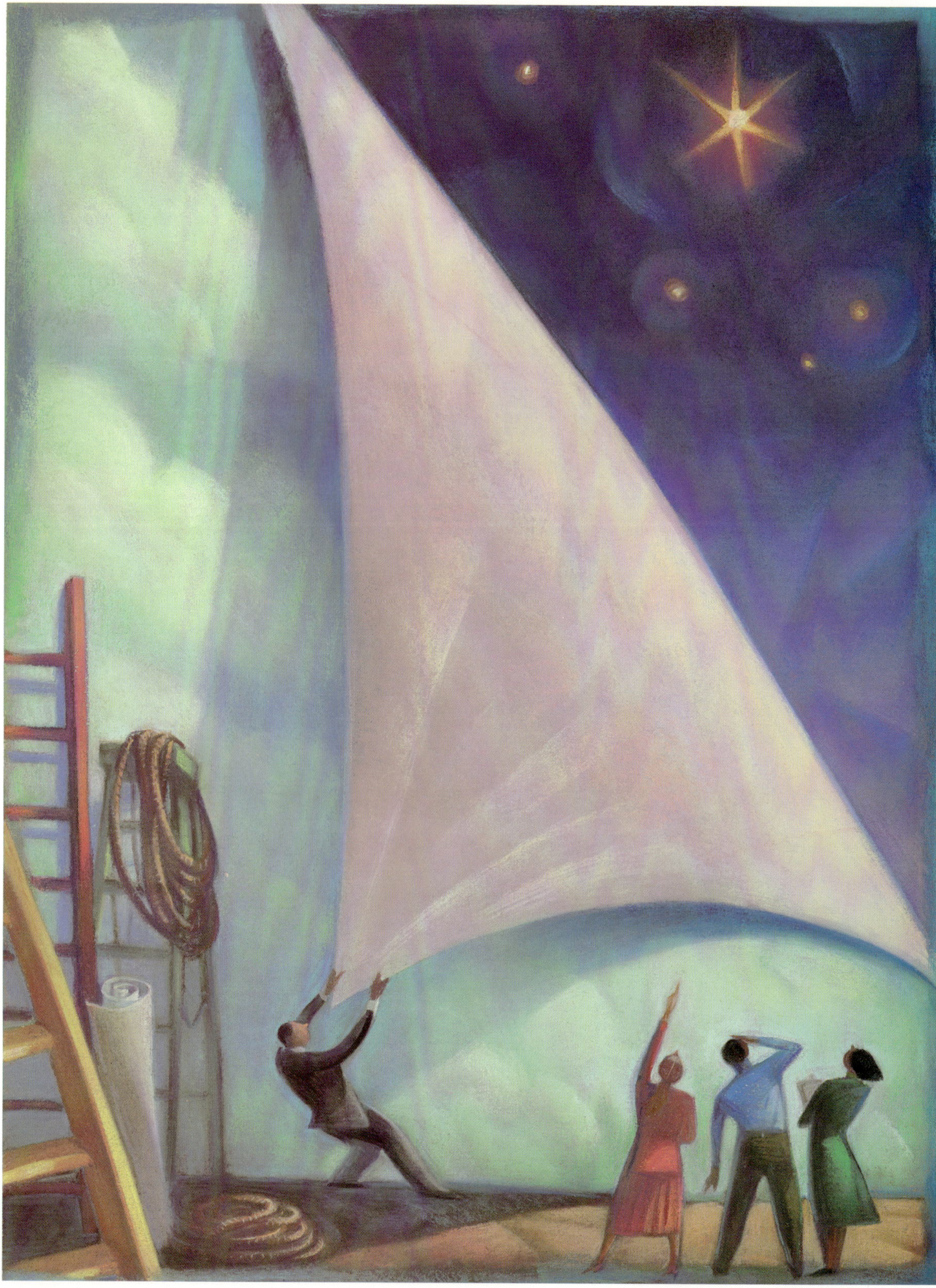

2. Inspire Commitment

Build insight and motivation so people focus their energy on goals that matter.

Leader As Coach

Jump-start

Inspiring commitment is most important when people:

- *Agree on a development need but don't do anything to address it.*
- *Spend their time pursuing development goals that are not important to getting their job done.*
- *Lose focus or shift from one learning objective to another without completing any of them.*
- *Wonder what they should develop.*
- *Prepare a development plan but do not take action on it.*
- *Seem content with their current level of skill and expertise.*

To inspire commitment:

- *Help people clarify their personal goals and values.*
- *Make sure you understand what matters to the people you coach.*
- *Help people find out what skills the organization values and why those skills are important.*
- *Make sure people get specific, relevant information about their performance.*
- *Help people formulate development goals that are consistent with organizational priorities.*

Strategy 2
INSPIRE COMMITMENT

Two of the toughest and most common questions about coaching and development are:
1. How do I motivate people to work on their development?
2. How do I make sure people work on the right things?

If you know the secret to these two questions, you can lead people to take personal responsibility for working on development priorities that matter to them and to your organization. Finding the secret requires that you turn each question inside out.

The truth about the first question is that you *can't* motivate people. However, you *can* tap into their natural motivations by applying the principle that people do things when they see a personal payoff. Approach your coaching like a gardener who does not try to motivate the plants to grow, but who seeks the right combination of sunlight, nourishment, and water to release the plant's natural growth. A gardener provides an environment conducive to growth, much as a coach creates the conditions in which personal motivation to develop will flourish. Thus, the inside-out version of the first question looks at enlightened self-interest:

1. HOW CAN I LEVERAGE THE PERSON'S NATURAL MOTIVATION TO GROW AND DEVELOP?

The truth about the second question is that everyone believes they already know the right things to work on. However, their point of view may be incomplete. They may not see the implications of their choices or they may lack critical information about their capabilities and what the organization expects from them. So the inside-out version of the second question becomes:

2. WHAT INFORMATION DOES THIS PERSON NEED IN ORDER TO UNDERSTAND THEIR CRITICAL DEVELOPMENT PRIORITIES?

CAPSULE PREVIEW

– *Cultivate insight into GAPS.*

– *Illuminate where people are starting from.*

– *Illuminate where people are going.*

– *Highlight gaps in their GAPS.*

– *Focus on critical priorities.*

– *Plan for development.*

Without the fuel of a personal payoff, people will not keep moving forward on their development. Without a destination that matters to the organization, their efforts may waste valuable time and resources. So to truly *Inspire Commitment,* make sure the development objectives are driven by the person's own goals and that they address organizational priorities as well. This alignment reinforces the two elements in the development partnership; both parties contribute and both parties gain.

The tactics in this chapter will help you get people moving and spur them in the right direction by showing you how to:
- Provide people with relevant information so they can make informed choices about what to develop.
- Stimulate people's natural curiosity to seek feedback and information from others.
- Unleash their natural motivation to develop by highlighting the discrepancies between where they are and where they want to go.
- Focus development on mutually beneficial areas by aligning their personal goals with organizational needs.
- Work together to devise a plan for development that targets important and realistic objectives.

> My task is not to motivate people to play great football. They are already motivated when they come to me. My challenge is simply not to demotivate them.
>
> *Lou Holtz*

Cultivate insight into GAPS

The first step to unleash people's desire and organizational support is to deepen people's insights about where they are now and where they want and need to be in the future. But people often have blind spots. They lack key information that prevents them from accurately perceiving both where they stand and where they want to go. You bring the discrepancy into sharper focus when you guide people toward **GAPS** information: their own **G**oals and **A**bilities as well as the **P**erceptions and **S**tandards of others.

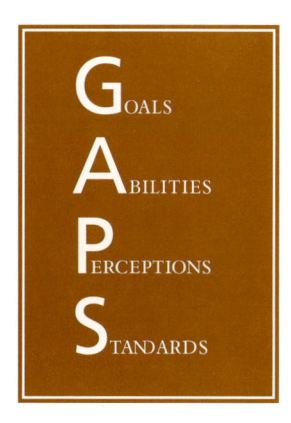

Goals
Abilities
Perceptions
Standards

GAPS Grid: Critical Information for Development

	Where the person is	Where the person is going	
	Abilities How they see themselves.	**Goals & Values** What matters to the person.	The person's view
	Perceptions How others see the person.	**Standards** What matters to others.	Others' views

Leader As Coach
Page 57

When people recognize gaps between these four kinds of information, they usually are energized to do something to resolve the difference, as in the following examples:

Reason for seeking development	**Gap that motivates development**
• Richard: "I always wanted to run a business unit, but I realized I needed to know a lot more about managing the financials."	• Richard's *goals* vs. his *abilities*.
• Anita: "I thought I was a good presenter, but I started to sense that sometimes I would lose my audience. Some people have said that my logic is hard to follow."	• Anita's self-evaluation of her *abilities* vs. others' *perceptions*.
• Carson: "I'm pretty good at working on my own, but my boss reorganized us into teams and I need to learn how to work more collaboratively."	• Carson's personal *abilities* vs. the organization's expectations and *standards*.
• Helen: "I want to move into a supervisory position, but other people aren't sure that I'm qualified."	• Helen's *goals* vs. others' *perceptions*.

Illuminate where people are starting from: Abilities and Perceptions

Information about people's abilities and how others perceive them helps them chart their starting location, like orienting themselves on a map emblazoned "You are here." *Abilities* include the person's view of their own capabilities, style, and performance. *Perceptions* convey how others view the person's capabilities, performance, style, motives, priorities, and values.

A full view of oneself includes the view through other lenses.

Eric helped Kris discover information on her abilities and others' perceptions after she complained that her boss wasn't supporting her desire to become a department manager.

"I don't get it," Kris exclaimed, "I have the right experience, a strong project management track record, and good relationships with my team. I think I'm every bit as qualified as some of the people who are already department managers."

Eric replied, "Then there must be reasons you don't know that explain why you aren't getting the opportunities you want. I'd be willing to help you think this through."

As a starting point, Kris and Eric categorized what they knew about her skills under three headings: very strong, solid, and needs work. Then Eric asked what she knew about how she was viewed by senior management. "I don't think they really appreciate what I have been able to accomplish with the resources I have. The politics are so thick that people rarely look at substance. I always deliver projects on time."

Trying to shift to a more objective analysis, Eric interrupted. "That could be a factor. But maybe if you really look at what they think of you, you can do something about it. Why don't we list what you already know about their views."

Kris responded, "I've heard that I'm a good team player. And people know I'll get the job done. I could pull out a copy of my last performance evaluation, but my ratings were pretty high across the board."

"At minimum, it sounds like you need another conversation with your boss. But ask about more than how you do the job and what results you get. Find out what he thinks of you as a leader. Then start to get more input from other senior managers. You work a lot with Matt in production, right? Any other ideas?"

"I could get feedback from my project sponsors whenever we meet key milestones," suggested Kris. "They actually work with me more than my boss does."

Then Eric and Kris brainstormed several questions she could ask them, such as, "I'm interested in becoming a better leader. What kinds of things do I do well and what could I do even better?"

It also occurred to Eric that because Kris had been in technical and project management roles her entire career, some of her leadership skills hadn't been put to the test. "Maybe an outside evaluation would give you a fresh opinion on how you stack up on management skills. Then you'd have another view to add to your boss's."

The following tactics, many of which Eric demonstrated in coaching Kris, help people understand where they are now.

Stimulate people to gather their own information. Your task is to equip and energize people so they embark on their own search, not to fill in all the gaps yourself. You can provoke their natural curiosity and launch them on their search for first-hand, unfiltered information by priming the pump with questions such as:
- How good do you think your skills are? What have other people said about your skills?
- How much do you really know about what your peers or your internal customers think of you?
- What can you do to be sure that you have a current, objective gauge on your abilities?

Offer objective feedback. One of the most valuable things you can do to help people develop is provide clear, honest, direct feedback.[6] But the headline on a story about development should read "Learner clamors for information," not "Coach delivers feedback."

When you provide feedback, keep in mind the following:
- Highlight the consequences of what you have observed so people understand why your feedback is important. Show them the logic path that connects what they did, how others reacted, and the likely consequences for them personally: "When you dominate staff meetings and push your own agenda so hard, people get irritated. You aren't likely to get the cooperation you want." Or, "You did a lot of advance work to understand the customer and then laid out a very convincing case in your presentation. You were able to persuade them that we could meet their needs, so we should be able to get more business from them in the future."
- If people aren't listening to your message, or they begin to defend themselves, you are probably trying too hard to convince them that you are right. Step back and frame your observations as an opinion for them to consider. "This is my view of you. I want to make sure you have a good picture of how I see you, then check around to see what other folks think." Your goal is to improve their understanding, not to provide them with "the truth."

If people are curious, they will come to you for feedback.

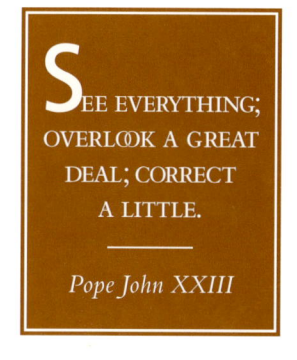

> SEE EVERYTHING; OVERLOOK A GREAT DEAL; CORRECT A LITTLE.
>
> *Pope John XXIII*

Teach people how to listen to feedback. Getting honest, comprehensive feedback is something of an art. Share the following advice with people to increase the chances they will get useful feedback from others:
- Let people know you are serious. "I'm asking for feedback because I really want to understand how people see me. That's the only way I can improve."
- Ask direct, specific questions. "What did you think of my presentation?" might yield general impressions, but "Tell me how well I identified and spoke to audience priorities" elicits more precise feedback.
- Keep asking, "What else?" until they tell you, "That's all."
- Don't defend or argue, just thank people for their input. They are doing you a favor, so don't make it difficult or unpleasant for them.

Treat feedback as a hypothesis to be tested.

Illustrate the range of sources. To prevent blind spots, people need to view themselves from many different angles.
- *Abilities* information can come from self-evaluation, performance evaluations, professional assessments using objective testing and skill simulations, or through observation and feedback from experts. Keep in mind that people who pay attention to their performance in a variety of situations are among the best judges of their own capabilities.
- *Perception* information can be obtained from anyone inside or outside the organization, including peers, bosses, senior management, customers, team members, and friends. People can ask for input through face-to-face conversations, multi-rater feedback surveys, informal feedback, and third-party interviews of coworkers. Vehicles that can provide anonymous and confidential information are often more candid than face-to-face methods.

Illuminate where people are going: Goals and Standards

When you clarify abilities and perceptions, you help people know where they stand right now. But people are also often in the dark about what is expected of them and where they should go next. One senior leader, reflecting on his development experiences, observed, "So much of the decision making about people is political. It's hard to tell what I should work on because I'm not sure what they're looking for."

Two types of information are essential to prioritize development efforts:
- *Goals and Values* are the motivators that energize and drive the person's behavior, including their interests, values, desires, work objectives, and career aspirations.
- *Standards* are the organization's success factors for the person, as defined by their roles and responsibilities, cultural norms, and other people's expectations.

Eric helped Kris clarify her development direction by first asking why she was interested in becoming department manager, then followed up exploring the company's standards and expectations for that position.

"I've always been pretty ambitious, and the DM job is my next challenge. I like having personal responsibility for things. I'm ready to start making more decisions about where we go and what we focus on."

"I suspect you could get some of those things from the job," Eric nudged her in a new direction. "But I'd like to hear about your leadership values, too. What do you want to accomplish as a leader? What do you stand for?"

"What do you mean?" Kris asked.

> If you would hit the mark, you must aim a little above it. Every arrow that flies feels the attraction of earth.
>
> *Henry Wadsworth Longfellow*

"Most leadership roles can be pretty turbulent. It helps to have a solid grounding in the things you believe in. This is your anchor when everything else is shifting, like a personal vision or mission statement. If you don't have one, you might want to put on paper what you want to be known for."

Kris paused a moment. "I haven't thought that through in any formal way, but I suppose I could. Now might be a good time to review Covey's *Seven Habits*[7] book."

"You should probably also talk to some DMs about their experiences in the job to find out what it has been like for them. The view from the inside isn't always the same as the view from the outside," Eric cautioned. "Maybe your boss would be willing to talk about his experiences. I've heard him comment that he had no idea what he was getting into."

Kris wasn't convinced. "I think I already have a good handle on the job requirements."

"I thought so, too, at first. But the job has changed a lot in the past few years. There's a lot more autonomy, but a lot fewer resources. The DMs have to do a lot of staff shuffling now. And they're responsible for more and more of the financial measures."

"I know that HR worked up some new DM requirements in the past year. It would be interesting to see what they came up with," she volunteered.

"Good idea. But make sure you get real life accounts of what it's like, too."

Eric used some of the following tactics to help Kris explore goals and standards:

Illustrate the range of sources.
- *Goals* and values information is available via personal reflection, writing a personal mission statement, values clarification exercises, career interest surveys, performance reviews, and annual goal-setting. Talk with people about their career ambitions, sort through what they like and dislike about work they have done, and steer them to people such as career counselors who can help them clarify their direction. Encourage them to keep and regularly review a list of the goals and values which are most important to them.
- *Standards* information is available from conversations with senior managers, job experts, statements of the corporate vision and strategy, marketplace analyses, competency models, team goals, individual performance expectations, and job descriptions.

Personalize organizational expectations.
Organizational values, missions, and strategies often remain vague and abstract, never affecting the actions and priorities of individual people. Coaches can translate these organizational standards into specific expectations.
- "Remember, Raj, that one of the objectives of our new mission statement is to empower our people more. That means you have to ask yourself on every decision you make: 'Can I push this down to the next level?'"
- "Lin, keep in mind that customers continually tell us that our responsiveness is our most significant advantage. We'll need better systems to make sure we keep this edge, so you might look for ways to rethink what we're doing at each step of the distribution process."

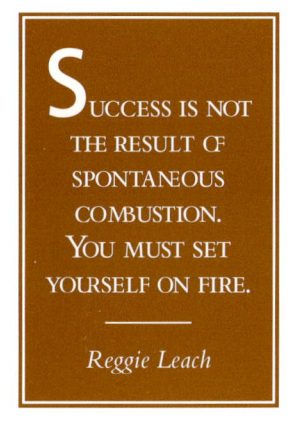

> SUCCESS IS NOT THE RESULT OF SPONTANEOUS COMBUSTION. YOU MUST SET YOURSELF ON FIRE.
>
> *Reggie Leach*

Stay in touch with emerging needs and potential future standards. Standards change as organizations and their environments change. If you keep current, you are better positioned to help your people work on the right things.
- Discuss your organization's mission and strategic plans. Clarify how strategies and competitive forces influence the competencies that your organization will value long term. "As we shift our administration to regional offices we will need people who know how to coordinate processes and who can quickly apply new information technology."
- Look to internal gurus and leaders for clues about the direction your organization is moving and the skills and abilities that will be most prized in the future. "As we try to be more integrated you'll have to work more collaboratively with teams of people from other groups. No one can continue to act the way they did when they were running their own show."
- Seek external perspectives about industry trends and competition from relevant periodicals, books, and conferences. "With the fierce competition in mid-range markets, people will have to be willing to challenge the old rules and come up with creative ways to meet customer expectations."

Highlight gaps in their GAPS

Next, turn the spotlight toward any significant gaps between people's *goals, abilities, perceptions,* and *standards*. People have a natural inclination to close these gaps. They can choose to do so by developing themselves, but they can also resolve a gap by ignoring the information that exposed the gap in the first place. You inoculate people against dismissing new information and you strengthen their personal ownership of their development needs when you:

Guide people to personalize the gaps. Ask questions to help people draw their own conclusions:
- What gaps do you see?
- Which are the most critical?
- Which ones are the most difficult for you to accept?
- Which gaps could make the biggest difference to you in the long run?
- What are you most interested in doing something about?

Offer an objective lens for viewing. Describe the gaps that you see without any criticism or value judgments. If you tell people what they should or shouldn't do, you'll tend to provoke defensiveness.
- *Goals* vs. *Perceptions*: "You want people to take your opinions seriously, yet they see you using humor to avoid conflict and disagreements."
- *Goals* vs. *Standards*: "Your objective this year is a 30% increase in sales revenue, but your manager is emphasizing the need to build profitability and leadership capabilities to sustain growth over the long haul."
- *Perceptions* vs. *Standards*: "The company mission statement emphasizes that everyone needs to be willing to challenge the status quo and help us reinvent ourselves. At the same time, you are perceived as cautious and overly consensus-seeking."
- *Abilities* vs. *Perceptions*: "There is no doubt that you are very bright, but few people have the chance to see that because you rarely speak up in meetings."

After evaluating her GAPS, Kris and her coach Eric consolidated the information into a grid to summarize the possible discrepancies:

GAPS Grid: Critical Information for Development

	WHERE THE PERSON IS	WHERE THE PERSON IS GOING	
	ABILITIES How they see themselves.	**GOALS & VALUES** What matters to the person.	THE PERSON'S VIEW
	PERCEPTIONS How others see the person.	**STANDARDS** What matters to others.	OTHERS' VIEWS

WHERE KRIS IS	WHERE KRIS WANTS TO GO	
Abilities: • Bright, motivated, and hard-working. • Very strong skills in software design, project management, communication, and problem solving. • Solid in strategic thinking and people skills. • Need better skills in financial management, leading cross-functional teams, and influencing peers and superiors.	**G**oals and Values: • Become a department manager in custom software or the software products group. • Have more autonomy and decision-making authority. Long term, run a piece of the business. • Use people skills and experience to foster a thriving, creative atmosphere within the team.	KRIS'S VIEW
Perceptions: • A talented manager who tends to look at the business primarily from an R&D perspective. Has a reasonable understanding of the market trends and competitive forces shaping the industry. • Not a powerful leader. Tends to wait for her management to set direction rather than articulating and supporting her own point of view. • Her modest impact and lack of cross-functional leadership experience have kept her out of consideration for a DM job.	**S**tandards: Department managers need to: • Be independent thinkers who can make good business decisions in the face of ambiguity. • Understand and address the issues facing the department and be responsive to input from marketing, manufacturing, engineering, and technical support. • Provide strong leadership, especially in cross-functional teams.	OTHERS' VIEWS

Focus on critical priorities

With gaps identified, work through the following analysis to identify the one or two highest priority development objectives:

1. **Choose the top personal incentives.** What do people care most about? People cannot work on everything at once, so ask them to identify their most compelling personal needs, considering both short-term and long-term objectives.
- Do they want to be more effective and efficient in their current job?
- Are they eager to prepare for a different job?
- Do they crave more personal satisfaction?
- Do they want to use their abilities to the best of their potential?
- Are they energized by staying on the technical cutting edge?

2. **Match with organizational incentives.** Look for the personal priorities that are compatible with organizational interests. Can the person's development in these areas:
- Build a capability that is critical to the organization's success?
- Help the organization make a critical change?
- Enhance competitive advantage?
- Improve customer service?
- Plug a hole in team performance?

Then, narrow the list to the development themes with the greatest win/win payback. The better the match, the stronger the personal and organizational commitment. For example:
- **Personal priority:** Be respected for technical skills.
- **Organizational incentive:** Develop new products.
- **Aligned development goal:** Develop technical capabilities that contribute to new products.

> The best motivation consists of getting a player to understand that his self-interest and the team's are inextricably bound up.
>
> Walter Kiechel III

3. CONSIDER THE ROI. An analysis of the return on investment for development will help determine if the objectives are worth doing. A clear sense of ROI often tempers desires in light of practical limits and helps people focus on the areas with sustainable payback over time.

Difficulty. Rate each objective as easy, moderate, or difficult to achieve. For example, converting a socially awkward analyst into the leader of a large team might be difficult, while training the analyst to do sophisticated market research might be relatively easy.

Cost. Assess the costs – in money, time, effort, and organizational support – for making the goal a reality. Even wonderful development ideas will wither like underfunded entrepreneurial ventures if they do not have sufficient investment.
- For example, well-rounded executive skills might be an exciting goal for a project manager, but this target will not make sense if the organization can't spare the money and effort required.
- Or perhaps your sales manager wants more marketing expertise, but the training costs and potential loss of her sales revenue would be too great to justify the investment.

Payback. Narrow the list to the objectives with the highest ROI by finding those where cost and effort are low relative to the payback.
- For example, a moderate-payback development goal that requires relatively little investment may well be worth the effort, while a high-investment one with moderate payback might not.

4. PICK ONE OR TWO TOP PRIORITIES. Choose those that make the most sense to begin working on *now*.

Plan for development

Too often, development planning ends when the objectives have been identified and put on paper. But don't stop now. The final step brings development to life by translating development priorities into an actionable plan.

Spend more time on development than on development planning.

One of the best ways to plan for development is to base the action steps on how people really develop, as referenced in the *Development FIRST* strategies. These strategies define what people can do, in partnership with others, to drive their own development:
- **F**ocus on priorities.
- **I**mplement something every day.
- **R**eflect on what happens.
- **S**eek feedback and support.
- **T**ransfer learning to next steps.

A plan for development can leverage the FIRST strategies if it meets the following criteria. Use this list as a reference to keep development on course throughout the process:

1. **Does the plan focus attention?** Even when people see where they need to go and are fired up to develop, they may be seduced off course because so many important things vie for their attention.
   - Does the plan focus on one or two specific priorities?
   - Is it accessible every day so people's development priorities and activities stay in the forefront of their thinking?
   - Does it anticipate distractions that are likely to draw them off course?

2. **Does the plan trigger daily action?** As in the fable of the tortoise and the hare, successful development resembles steady persistence rather than splashy spurts of activity.

Five minutes of focused attention each day can yield more development than a five-day, or even a five-week, all-out sprint. Yet what are the most common entries in development plans? Take a two-week training course, read a leadership book, and review the plan in six months. Books and courses are fine for building new skills and knowledge, but they are inadequate for sustaining regular development activity. Does the plan:
- List times, situations, and people who will trigger new behavior? For example, a plan might remind someone to practice influencing skills every time they talk with their team leader, when a key topic is mentioned, or if they get a certain kind of request.
- Remind them to keep plodding through the routine aspects of development? While growth can be exciting, the day-to-day reality of learning something new often feels like drudgery.

3. **Does the plan capture new learning?** People who reflect on their development actions can consolidate their lessons, identify themes and patterns in their progress, and make sure they are learning the right things. Does the plan:
- Designate when and how they will take time for reflection?
- Provide a vehicle for keeping a learning record that will track and summarize what they have learned?
- Prompt them to diagnose the barriers that might be impeding their progress?

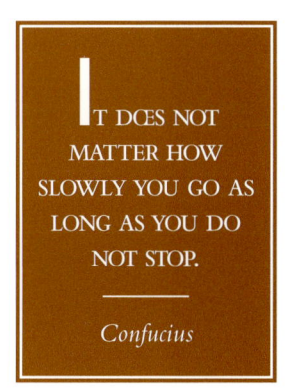

> **It does not matter how slowly you go as long as you do not stop.**
>
> *Confucius*

4. **Does the plan track and sustain progress?** As people develop, they often shift perspectives on their starting point, their current position, and their destination. They need to plan how they will get accurate, current information on where they stand relative to their goal. They also need to plan who will give them assistance and support.
- Who will they talk to for pertinent feedback?
- How can they measure progress toward their goals, not just goal attainment?
- How will they procure resources and access to new opportunities?
- Who can provide them with encouragement?

5. **Does the plan live and breathe?** Plans need to be flexible so they can accommodate changes in GAPS and help learners take advantage of new tactics and opportunities.
- How will the plan adjust to changing circumstances?
- How will the plan adapt to changing competency levels? If people are improving, the plan should crank up standards, fine-tune goals, and change tactics to keep people focused and challenged. If people do not change as hoped, the plan needs to recalibrate priorities and tactics and get them back on track.
- How and when will the plan be reviewed?

People should base revisions on significant new information rather than whim, convenience, or an unexpected chance to work on a less important area.

The best path across the mountains is often not the one envisioned from the valley.

Tips to help you inspire commitment

- Ask people to list the skills and characteristics they believe are most important for their jobs.
- Invite people to participate in a professional assessment that is focused on development.
- Create opportunities for people to get feedback via a multi-rater questionnaire.
- Discuss with people the development priorities they gleaned from recent feedback.
- Encourage people to clarify their career goals through counseling and reading.
- Share information on requirements for jobs related to the one they currently hold.
- Distribute documents on customers' corporate strategies, the competition, and industry trends.
- Establish a regular process for sharing specific performance feedback with members of your team.
- Invite people to discuss their goals and plans with colleagues in similar circumstances.
- Push people to limit and focus their plan for development to things they can work on immediately.
- Challenge people to consider their real development barriers, such as time and resource limits.

In addition, the following tips might be useful for people in these coaching groups:

1. Set the standard.
- Specify the ways in which important standards are not being met.
- Clarify the risks of not changing.
- Discuss how required changes link to people's personal goals and desires.
- Express empathy for the challenges the person is facing.

2. Set new direction.
- Explain the history and rationale behind the new standards.
- Show appreciation for the ways in which people have met the old standards.
- Provide information on trends and changes to stir up dissatisfaction with the status quo.
- Establish a vehicle to continually clarify and reiterate the need for a new direction.
- Highlight existing skills that people can leverage for future success.
- Focus on possibilities and opportunities, not just limitations.

3. Set free.
- Ask people to articulate their dreams and aspirations.
- Promote breakthrough goals that stretch people well beyond their comfort zone.
- Create excitement by talking about new applications for high level skills.
- Articulate the organizational incentives for achieving significant development objectives.

Personal action steps

Master the basics. As you apply this strategy, make sure you have a solid foundation in:
- Active listening skills.
- Discussing performance feedback.

How will you work to inspire commitment in the person you are coaching?
- How well does the person understand their GAPS?
- What new information do they need? How can you ensure they obtain it?
- How can you make sure the organizational rationale for their development objective makes sense to them?
- How closely are their objectives supported by their personal goals and values?

What have you learned so far about yourself as a coach?
- What insights do you want to remember from this chapter?
- What one or two things would make the most difference in your coaching?

Where will you begin to take action?
- What ideas are you going to try first?
- What will you incorporate into your plans for coaching others?
- What else do you need for your own development?

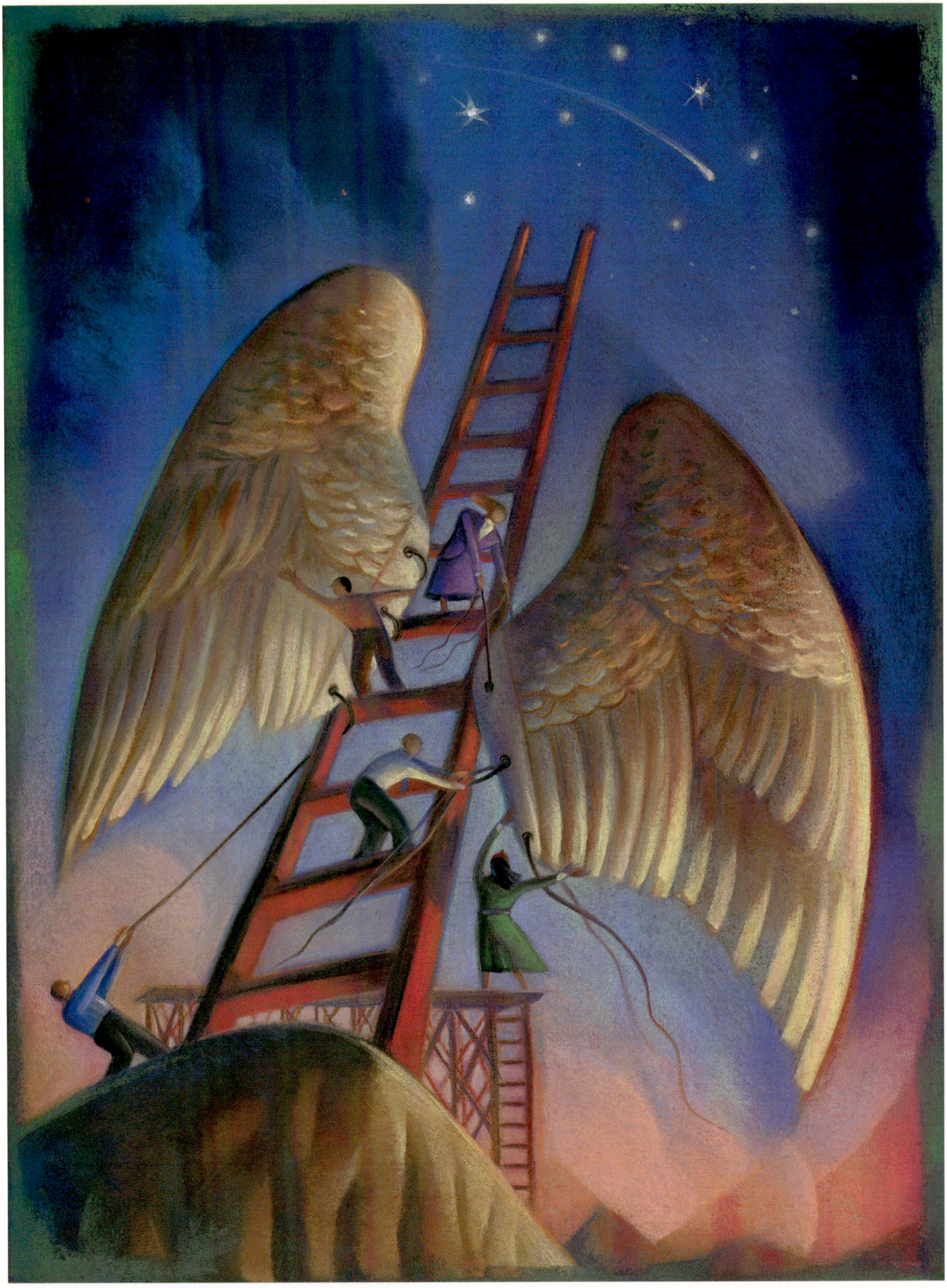

3. Grow Skills

Build new competencies to ensure
people know how to do what is required.

Leader As Coach

Jump-start

Growing skills is most important when people:

- *Have never had the chance to acquire a skill they need.*
- *Need to upgrade their skills to meet new standards or emerging expectations.*
- *Have solid skills but need advanced knowledge and techniques.*
- *Are motivated to do well but their performance is still below par.*
- *Are eager to develop but do not know what to do first.*

To grow skills:

- *Connect people with tutors and mentors who have the desired skill.*
- *Find coursework targeted at skill-building and practice.*
- *Help people find practical, relevant books and readings.*
- *Broker opportunities for people to observe the skill being used effectively.*
- *Create opportunities that stretch people to learn something new.*
- *Teach people how to learn from their successes and failures.*

Strategy 3
GROW SKILLS

Leaders often equate coaching and development with teaching people how to do new things. Almost by default, they turn to coursework, tutoring, and reading. Although new knowledge and skills are often necessary, don't automatically assume that you need this strategy. In many cases, people already have the skills or the knowledge they need, but they lack the trust, motivation, or techniques to apply new skills. Determine if they need to focus on *learning* or on *doing*; identify which key will unlock each person's performance.

With this in mind, answer two questions to decide if you should embark on building new skills or if another strategy is needed:
1. Does the person lack the skills completely or are they just not applying them?
2. If they need new skills, are the skills clearly defined?

Liken the first question to asking, "Does this computer need new software or do we just have to launch the application?" A person who needs new skills is like a computer that can't perform because it doesn't have the software. Use the tactics in *Grow Skills* with these people. A person who has skills but doesn't use them, or doesn't use them consistently, is like a computer with up-to-date software that isn't deployed well. You can use the next strategy, *Promote Persistence,* to help these people apply their skills consistently.

The second question is akin to, "What software does the computer need?" Only certain software will meet your specifications. It is the same with people development. The learning method must match the need. If not, even excellent resources – university-based executive programs, internal training courses, mentoring – will be squandered.

If you answer both questions affirmatively – the person needs new skills *and* you are clear about which new skills they need – read on in this chapter. If not, review the other strategies to clarify goals, encourage people to commit to development, and help people put their skills into action.

CAPSULE PREVIEW

– *Experience can be a lousy teacher.*

– *Find the best ways to learn new skills.*

– *Orchestrate learning opportunities and resources.*

– *Take advantage of coachable moments.*

– *Teach people how to learn for themselves.*

Learning is not the same as doing.

EXPERIENCE CAN BE A LOUSY TEACHER

Most people take it on faith that "experience is the best teacher." Indeed, if you reflect on your past, you will no doubt confirm that your experiences have provided invaluable lessons. Although exposure to new experiences creates opportunity for new learning, experience alone is rarely the best teacher. Consider how relying on experience to learn new skills can fall short:

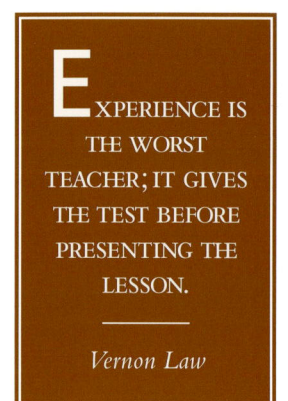

> **People might not learn the right lesson.** Experience can petrify bad practices into habits, making the chore of development even more difficult. Experience can even stifle good behaviors. For example, a leader exposed to a difficult turnaround experience might learn to be tough and directive instead of participative. Someone else might "learn from experience" that they shouldn't ask questions or volunteer new ideas in meetings.
>
> Even more troublesome, experience alone cannot distinguish highly skilled performers from those who are not. One researcher found that both successful and unsuccessful managers had faced similar development challenges. She concluded that "developmental events do not lead to success in any straightforward or predictable way."[8] More is necessary than experience alone.

> EXPERIENCE IS THE WORST TEACHER; IT GIVES THE TEST BEFORE PRESENTING THE LESSON.
>
> *Vernon Law*

Experience is slow and inefficient. Experience is rarely proactive, strategic, or focused. People who proceed solely by trial and error, or who do not know what they are supposed to learn, might end up having the same year of experience ten times over. Broad experiences rarely zero in on the most important lessons.

The right experiences are in limited supply. Many leaders cite leading a turnaround or start-up situation as the best lesson they ever had. These are relatively rare opportunities in most organizations. Imagine that you want 50 people, or even five people, to learn something quickly. Creating on-the-job experiences for each of them is virtually impossible.[9] In addition, work assignments and opportunities are usually based on *doing* well rather than *learning* well; people are given opportunities because someone believes they can deliver right now. Commitments to development aside, the immediate interests of the enterprise usually prevail over granting someone a learning experience.

None of this should imply that experience cannot teach people. To the contrary, this is to remind you that experience needs to be used wisely as part of a complete C&D strategy.

The rest of this chapter focuses on how you can make experience a good teacher, by ensuring that people:
• Find the right experiences for acquiring new skills.
• Learn the right lessons from those experiences.
• Learn quickly.

Find the best ways to learn new skills

People don't learn to play the piano through reading and they don't learn how to fly by tinkering with flight controls. So, what is the best way for people to learn new things?

Match the method to the need. You can help people find the best prescription for learning by pointing them to options as varied as books, seminars, work experiences, and mentoring from others. But how do you decide? Think of what you already know about how people learn different subjects:
- Engineering, accounting, and other fact-based topics through books, classes, and on-the-job instruction from experts.
- Sales, communications, and interpersonal skills through role-playing, observing experts in action, and hands-on practice.
- Business and marketing strategies, organizational savvy, and many facets of leadership through case study, discussion, and analysis of real-world examples.
- Personal values and vision through introspection, case study, simulations, and dialog.

For each of these – facts, skills, strategies, and values – real-world experience is essential to deepen insight and forge sound judgment about how and when to use what they have learned. In addition, two principles can help people make the most of their experience:

1. Space the practice. No one develops competence in just one lesson, so encourage people to pace their learning. New behaviors and new ways of thinking assimilate best when acquired in manageable bits spaced across time, like taking piano lessons each week and practicing for 30 minutes a day.

2. Promote active experimentation. Regardless of the methods, skills never develop fully if they are only used in a single setting. People need to try new skills on for size, experiment with them, and adapt them to different situations. When people try new things in different ways, they solidify their understanding of what really works and prepare themselves to use the skills smoothly in a variety of circumstances.

Orchestrate learning opportunities and resources

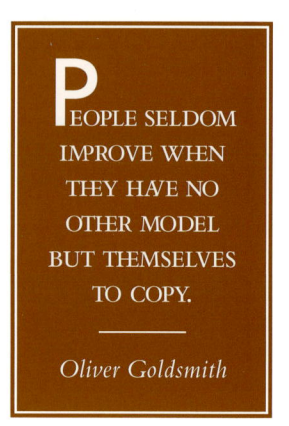

To connect people with the right learning experiences:

Broker resources. Like a broker who finds products for buyers, you can link people who need particular skills with resources, such as training programs, career centers, or experts in other departments. Even if you don't know the resource yourself, you might know someone who does. For example, since organizational savvy is learned better from a mentor than from a book, you can network to track down a mentor on the topic.

Stay fresh. Avoid getting stuck in a rut, such as just pulling out the same old training course catalog. Keep your eyes open for new ways of learning by surveying your network to identify experts and to glean testimonials about great new resources. To find new angles for skill-building, look for cutting-edge books, find powerful new courses, and refer to catalogs of development suggestions, such as the *Successful Manager's Handbook*.[10]

Create room for learning. With time in short supply, people often postpone or abandon their intentions to pick up a new skill. It is quicker and easier to do things the old way than to stumble through something new. Even experts who want to be mentors often try to save time by doing the work themselves rather than teaching others to do it. Yet both experts and learners must trade short-term pain for long-term gain. Take some of the pressure off and help people over these initial hurdles by diverting some of their tasks and responsibilities to others. Or, let them know that it is OK to shift their focus – temporarily! – if they need some room while learning a new skill.

> People seldom improve when they have no other model but themselves to copy.
>
> *Oliver Goldsmith*

Keep your eyes open for new ways of learning.

Take Advantage of Coachable Moments

Experiences deliver the greatest learning punch when people try new things and then reflect to extract maximum learning from their experiences. If you allocate 5% of your attention to C&D, you will be ready to pounce when people are ripe for learning, such as the following coachable moments:

Coaches look for the coachable moment.

Surprising successes. Victories often tempt people and their coaches to celebrate and move on to the next challenge. Go ahead and rejoice. But don't run off before you review what happened so the person can replicate, or even improve, performance in the next round.

1. *Diagnose the cause.* What factors within the person's control contributed to the outcome, including their skills, preparation, and attitude? What factors outside their control contributed? Help them give themselves credit when it is due.
2. *Find the lesson.* Decide what the person should repeat, improve, or avoid at the next opportunity. What else can they do to increase the odds of success or minimize risks?
3. *Transfer the lesson to a new situation.* Identify at least two similar situations or new opportunities where the lessons can be applied.

Failures and disappointments. Failures evoke both discouragement and curiosity, as people contend with what went wrong and why. Yet efforts to console people with a supportive comment, such as "Don't worry; you'll do better next time," gloss over the person's true feelings and squander a learning opportunity. Instead, express your support by listening to their feelings and helping them gain a new perspective on what happened by following the three steps outlined above.

Requests for advice or opinions. When you get questions like "How did that go?" or "What should I do?" or "What do you think?," you probably reflexively toss back advice. Instead, hold your comments in check and determine how to use this opportunity to help people glean their own lessons from the situation.

1. ***Find out what they really want.*** Are they seeking advice, encouragement, or permission? Do they want your suggestions or do they have some ideas they want to explore with you?
2. ***Check their thinking first.*** Explore their own answers to their questions before sharing your views. What options do they see? What are the pros and cons of each one?
3. ***Add your own ideas.*** Complete the picture by discussing other options that you see.
4. ***Define next steps.*** Finally, pin down what they will do next. Does the outcome of your discussion meet their need or should they look further? How are they going to use what you have discussed? What will they do to take their exploration the next step?

> KNOW WHEN TO SPEAK; FOR MANY TIMES IT BRINGS DANGER TO GIVE THE BEST ADVICE TO KINGS.
>
> *Robert Herrick*

Even brilliant coaching techniques can backfire if the timing is wrong. As you look for coachable moments, be sure to avoid these circumstances when coaching might not be appropriate:

- People need praise or encouragement, not instruction or advice.
- The setting is wrong, such as in a public situation or when you are pressed for time.
- They have already filled their capacity for new lessons. Remember that people learn in bite-sized doses.
- People are overly stressed or preoccupied about something else.
- You are unprepared or preoccupied with other things.

Make sure, however, that you are not letting people off the hook too easily. There is no such thing as perfect timing.

Teach people how to learn for themselves

To repeat a refrain that fits every coaching strategy: Download the learning process to others so they have the tools in their own hands.

Coaches extend the lessons of experience.

Coach people to Focus – Implement – Reflect. This applies the first three steps of *Development FIRST* to working on a specific skill.
- **Focus.** Encourage people to scan their daily schedule of activities to find the best situations to learn or practice something new. By focusing on the best learning opportunities, they can learn more quickly and efficiently. For example, any group meeting would be an opportunity to observe influencing skills; a project review would be an opportunity to ask an expert for a few tips.
- **Implement.** Make sure they take full advantage of each learning opportunity, whether observing others or putting a new skill into action.
- **Reflect.** After they have implemented what they have learned they can extract the lessons through reflection. What did they do well and what did they omit? How did the circumstances affect their success? To solidify the lesson, they can plan what they want to repeat or change next time. Each round of the focus-implement-reflect cycle accumulates new lessons on how to learn.

Broaden the domain of learning situations. Help people knock off their own blinders to look beyond the obvious sources of new skills, such as coursework and books.
- Urge them to view everyday circumstances, such as meetings and customer visits, as chances to pick up new insights and techniques.
- Point them to internal and external experts, and encourage them to network to find out who knows the things that they want to learn. Discuss how they can gain access to mentors and role models.

Help people identify learning moments. Just as you need to be prepared for spontaneous coachable moments, learners need to be prepared to take advantage of unexpected learning opportunities.
- Situations that stretch the limits of people's comfort zone are ripe with learning potential. Yet at such times, people are more prone to panic than to ask, "What can I learn from this?" To help them pierce through the anxiety and carve out a lesson, ask them to identify how they feel when they are tested. Do they have a knot in their stomach? Are their palms sweaty? These cues should become reminders that they have a first-rate chance to learn something new.
- Prompt people to be opportunistic. For example, if they are learning new conflict resolution skills, they should watch for disagreement and then observe how others manage the situation. Or, if they see someone demonstrate a skill that they admire, they can ask for on-the-spot counsel.

Tips to help you grow skills

- Help people get learning tips from coworkers who have recently faced similar learning challenges.
- Ask a skilled coworker to meet with the person and discuss how they would approach a given situation.
- Talk with colleagues about courses, books, and other training resources they have found particularly helpful.

In addition, the following tips might be useful for people in these coaching groups:

1. Set the standard.
- Enroll people in skill-building courses targeted one level above their current expertise.
- Find books that discuss practical uses of the new skill.
- Network to find situations where people can observe others using the skill effectively.
- Assign a tutor who can teach the basics.
- Give people permission to take risks and try new things.
- Avoid throwing people into situations that require significantly better skills than they currently possess.
- Reinforce the reason meeting the standard is critical.

2. Set new direction.
- Enroll people in courses that emphasize adapting to changing situations through new skills.
- Find peers in similar circumstances who can offer support and advice.
- Connect people with advisors who can demonstrate the real world application of the new skill.
- Acknowledge the difficulty of changing to a new set of skills.
- Talk with people about how well their old skills will transfer into new situations and what alternatives they have.
- Reinforce the reasons why the new direction is important.

3. Set free.
- Link people with internal experts for counsel and mentoring.
- Enroll people in specialized classes conducted by experts.
- Allow time to study the state-of-the art and to experiment with new approaches.
- Invest in their consultation with external gurus.
- Reinforce the long-term value of honing skills and developing mastery.

Personal action steps

Master the basics. As you apply this strategy, make sure you have a solid foundation in:
- Knowing where to find resources and learning opportunities for specific development needs.

How will you enable the person you are coaching to grow skills?
- How convinced are you that the person needs to acquire the new skill? If they have already had the opportunity to learn the skill but are not using it regularly on the job, skip to the next strategy.
- What kind of learning opportunities are best suited to their needs? How will you help them find these learning opportunities?
- Which people in your organization can be resources to help individuals learn the new skill?
- Which resources are not available in your organization and what will it take to find them elsewhere?
- What investment of time and resources is required? How will you secure this investment?

What have you learned so far about yourself as a coach?
- What insights do you want to remember from this chapter?
- What one or two things would make the most difference in your coaching?

Where will you begin to take action?
- What ideas are you going to try first?
- What will you incorporate into your plans for coaching others?
- What else do you need for your own development?

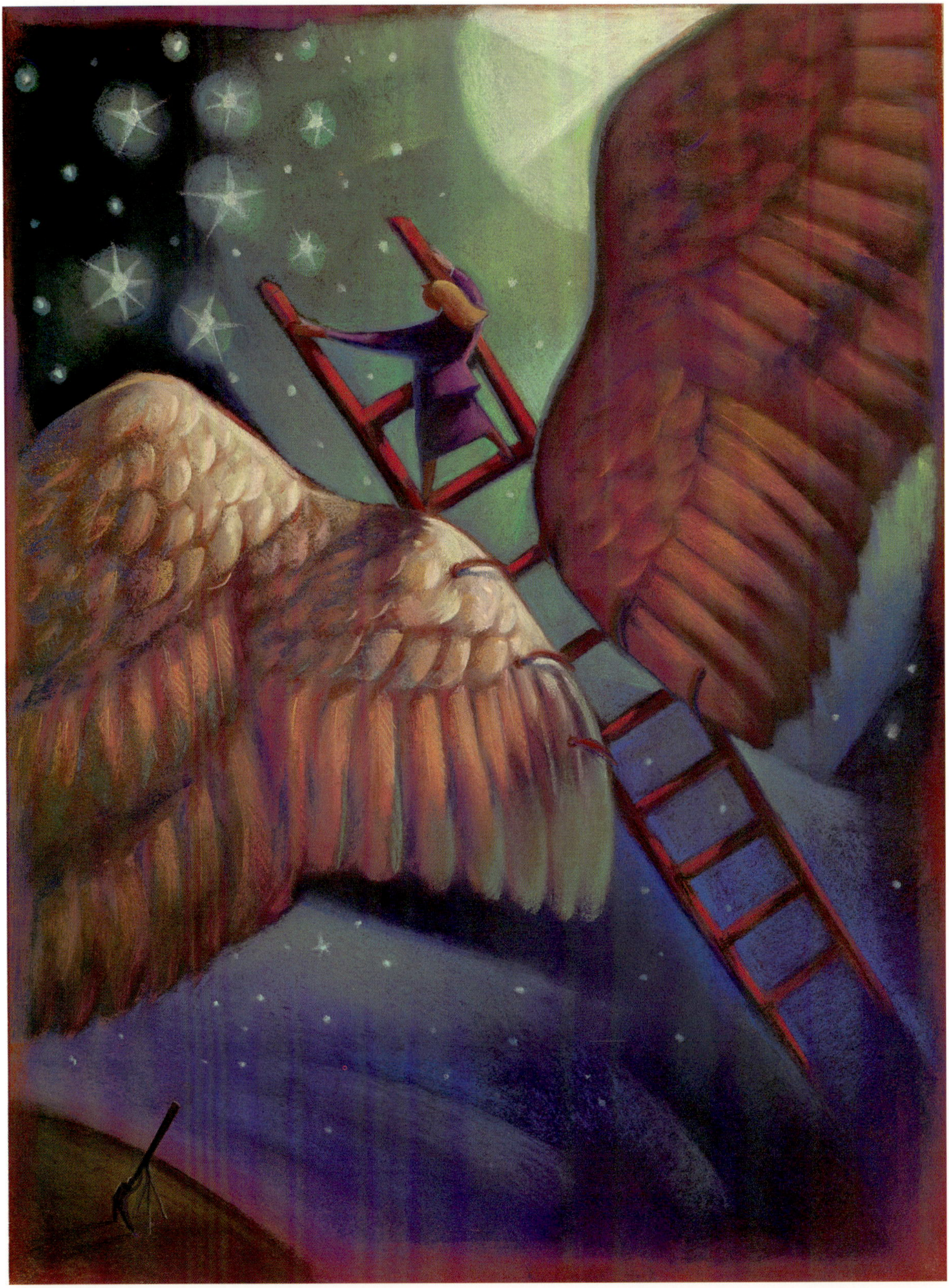

4. Promote Persistence

Build stamina and discipline to make sure learning lasts on the job.

Leader As Coach

Jump-start

Promoting persistence is most important when people:

- Stay stuck in their old habits.
- Make initial changes but then slip back into old behaviors.
- Do not take advantage of opportunities to use their new skills.
- Are reluctant to take risks or try something new.
- Plateau or get bored with the mundane aspects of learning.

To promote persistence:

- Periodically review people's goals and ask about their progress to refresh commitment.
- Set realistic expectations for progress; make sure other people in the organization have realistic expectations as well.
- Encourage people to keep pushing their comfort zone on new behaviors.
- Find new places and ways for people to apply their skills.
- Teach people how to get feedback for themselves.
- Provide ongoing feedback that recognizes and rewards their progress.
- Build their confidence to take appropriate risks.

Strategy 4
Promote Persistence

"Use it or lose it." Once people acquire a new skill, those are the choices. Unless they are put to use, knowledge and ability are dormant assets with little payback.

People may be willing to try a new behavior off-line, such as in a classroom or a dry run, yet balk when they must "go live" in the real world with real consequences. This is one reason why real change often fails to materialize even when people have acquired a new skill. But the goal of development is action, not merely insight or a course certificate. When people have mastered the flight simulator, they need to climb into the cockpit, strap in for takeoff, and take the plane for a ride.

Even when people take flight, the question lingers, "Will the changes last?" This skepticism is well founded. Changes often *don't* last because they are not backed with stamina and discipline. Only through practice and repeated applications can people make new skills a solid part of their repertoire.

You can make sure learning is applied and lasts on the job by helping people:
- Find opportunities to apply their new skills many times, in many places, and in many ways, so they solidify and sharpen their skills.
- Manage the routine aspects of development so they persist when they hit plateaus or when tasks become tedious.
- Feel comfortable enough with risk-taking that they don't panic or give up.
- Stretch their capabilities to achieve their full potential.
- Get excited about continuous development.

Capsule Preview

– *Be a talent agent.*

– *Manage the mundane.*

– *Fight fear of failure.*

– *Break the habit cycle.*

– *Challenge people to peak performance.*

> The great end of life is not knowledge but action.
>
> *Thomas Henry Huxley*

Be a talent agent

People will not excel at flying without the chance to exercise their wings. In the preceding strategy, *Grow Skills,* you brokered people and situations that had something to teach the learner. This strategy, *Promote Persistence,* reverses the challenge. Like a talent agent who finds work for clients, you must now identify people and situations that need the learner's skills.

Let people test their wings. Some new capabilities meet obvious needs; people with those skills will be consumed immediately by pent-up demand. Other people's talents must be showcased and promoted. Therefore, the talent agent has two primary tasks:
- Match talent with needs and opportunities.
- Market and promote people's talent so they get opportunities they would not have without your support.

As you promote persistence, remember that people are still engaged in the process of development. Your goal is to find hands-on tasks where they can experiment and apply what they have learned, not to find totally new assignments or to vault people out of their current jobs.

Match talent with needs. "I need experience to get the job, but I can't get experience until I have the job." Your advocacy can spring people from this trap. At the same time, because people can't infinitely add new challenges to their already full schedules, you may need to help them download or defer some of their responsibilities to make room for developmental tasks.

Scan for needs.
- Actively network so you are aware of demand for specific skills. Keep your finger on the pulse of the organization.
- Tell human resources staff and your colleagues that you are interested in hearing about opportunities. Periodically repeat your request as a reminder of your interest.

Create matches. Plug people in where they are needed, inside your department and elsewhere. Look for win/win situations, where the learner can solidify expertise as well as offer a valued service:
- A technician who has been building breadth in software applications could work with the sales team to expand its use of new client management software.
- An engineering manager who has been learning financial skills could help a struggling unit manager diagnose problems in the manufacturing budget.
- A project coordinator who has learned group process facilitation could be matched with a task force that is bogged down in details.

Market and promote talent. In any organization, the people with good reputations get the best opportunities. You gain visibility for people and plug them into the resource pool through your recommendations. Moreover, your personal endorsement boosts people's self-confidence and commitment to succeed.
- Because you are recommending an unknown commodity – new people with emerging capabilities – back your endorsements with evidence that the person is ready for the new challenge. Your reputation and credibility are on the line as well, so be thoughtful about your endorsements. Do not recommend someone unless you know they are ready for the challenge.
- With time, an organization accumulates a collective perception of people and their capabilities: "Joe is just a bean counter" or "Give your detail work to Sally." You often need some PR and spin control to spring people free from the old perceptions. "Joe is not just doing routine accounting anymore. He is becoming a topnotch project manager." "Sally has been expanding her scope recently. She is developing into our resident expert on scenario planning."

Manage the mundane

> **N**OTHING IN THE WORLD CAN TAKE THE PLACE OF PERSISTENCE. TALENT WILL NOT... GENIUS WILL NOT... EDUCATION WILL NOT... PERSISTENCE AND DETERMINATION ALONE ARE OMNIPOTENT.
>
> *Calvin Coolidge*

When people find the opportunities to apply and refine their emerging skills, they may seek shortcuts to make things happen quicker or easier. But there are no shortcuts: New habits are forged only with conscious effort and repeated practice. One manager in the throes of developing a new skill complained, "I feel like I'm trying to write with my left hand. I just want to pick up the pen with my right hand and do what I have always done. Does it have to be this hard?" Yes, trying something new can be that hard.

After an initial spurt of success, people often discover that additional gains in performance are far less dramatic. But they won't master the new skill unless they stick with it. Even world-class cellist Pablo Casals, at the age of 80, continued to practice four or five hours a day. When asked if he thought such rigor was still necessary, he replied, "I think so. I'm beginning to make some progress."

How can you help bolster people's motivation when development becomes dull or just plain hard work?

Keep them focused. Here is one place your earlier efforts to *Inspire Commitment* really pay off. Revisit people's personal goals to recharge their spirits and boost their energy. Reinforce the organization's need for their new skills.

Keep their development on your scope. Show that their goals are high on your agenda. Whenever you talk about business goals or financial performance, discuss their development progress as well. Find out if they need any help or if they are running into barriers.

Introduce new twists. Novelty, even in small ways, helps keep development fresh. For example, look for ways to test their skills at a different task or with a different person.

Get others on board. Development occurs in a social context. Other people can energize persistence if you let them know how to help. Assist them in setting realistic expectations about the person's learning process and suggest how they might offer encouragement and freedom to try new things.

Reward progress, not just results. Many people falter when their initial steps aren't noticed. A marketing executive at a large consumer foods company, who had observed considerable developmental effort on the part of his regional director, was asked if he had told the director that he was pleased with her progress. "No, she's just rounding first base at this point. I wouldn't want her to think she was almost home." The director was craving support and even a hint that her efforts were making a difference. But the executive presumed that a pat on the back would cause her to slack off. In fact, a good cheering section would have let her know she was heading in the right direction and encouraged her to keep running.

> Reward progress, not just results.

Fight fear of failure

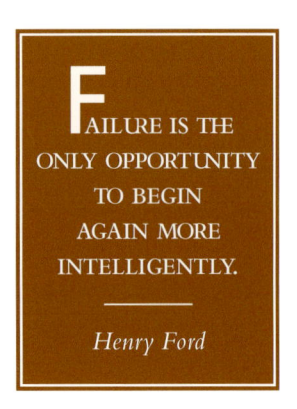

> **F**ailure is the only opportunity to begin again more intelligently.
>
> *Henry Ford*

People often need a boost over the hump between new knowledge and new behavior because trying new skills makes them feel awkward, frustrated, or vulnerable. Before they will take a big leap, they have to turn the corner from believing "I'm not ready yet" to "I'm ready to give it a try."

You help them turn this corner by showing that you believe in their ability to succeed. You can also cultivate a safe haven where the costs of failure are minimized and the value of experimentation is highlighted. When people believe they might succeed, and trust that they won't get burned for trying, they are much more willing to try.

Give them permission to be a novice. Change is often hard simply because people have to shed their old habits and act in ways that do not come naturally. Veteran performers who are used to doing things well now have to struggle with making basic mistakes and feeling like amateurs. Let people know that almost everyone feels some reluctance and apprehension when stepping out of their comfort zone. You expect to see clumsiness at first, so give them permission to make mistakes, as long as they learn from them. You can even position their early efforts as experiments to help them test the waters without assuming the full risks.

Build their confidence. Confident people are more willing to take risks. A mistake or two won't rattle them, because they believe they can do better the next time.

- ***Convey confidence in their ability.*** Your optimism can become a self-fulfilling prophecy. Consider the day that Larry Bossidy, AlliedSignal's CEO, interrupted Daniel Burnham, head of the aerospace division, in the middle of a presentation: "I was about 10% finished when Larry smiled and patted me on the shoulder," recalls Burnham. "He said, 'I know you can do it, even if you think you can't. I've got a lot of confidence in you.' End of discussion."[11] That support inspired Burnham to move forward quickly rather than spend his energy covering his position.
- ***Cite past successes.*** When you can, back up your confidence in people with evidence that demonstrates they can meet the test, even in the face of uncertain odds. For example, list the parallels between their current challenge and situations they have handled successfully in the past.
- ***Help people take responsibility for their successes.*** People who attribute past successes to luck or circumstances are often reluctant to take risks because they believe the outcome is outside their control. But when they link success to personal skill and effort, they trust their ability to succeed in the future. Show people the cause-and-effect connections, such as, "You won that customer over because you researched your topic, discovered his concerns, and honed your message to meet his needs," and "Your project is running smoothly because of all the work you've done to keep everyone informed."

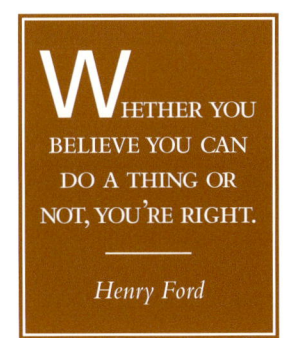

> WHETHER YOU BELIEVE YOU CAN DO A THING OR NOT, YOU'RE RIGHT.
>
> *Henry Ford*

Provide a safety net. With a safety net, people can vault forward knowing they won't get hurt.
- "I think you can do this yourself, but if you get stuck, you can come to me."
- "Why don't you invite the sales manager to the customer meeting, just in case questions come up that you can't answer."
- "I'll let Bill know this is the first time you have presented the monthly results so he isn't too hard on you."

Find the right-sized challenges. Challenges that are too big or too small do not provide realistic tests of what people are capable of doing; the results are almost predetermined. But when people succeed at mid-sized challenges, where they stretch their skills to face moderate risk, they gain new information about the effectiveness of their new skills. Of course, heroic efforts and difficult assignments also help people learn, but you can't make sink-or-swim your standard approach. You would rarely want to send someone fresh from a course on "Effective Speaking" into a major presentation with the CEO.

Gradually raise the bar. Remember that the discrepancy between where people are and where they want to be can generate tension that can motivate. Steadily raising the bar encourages continuous improvement. Pace the increments so you push their comfort zone without sending them over the edge. Regular investment in small change produces a high return over time.

Visualize the success. Suggest that people picture themselves successfully handling an upcoming situation, as if they were watching a film of themselves. To build confidence, they should envision themselves moving through their entire performance, mastering any challenges that arise.

Help people prepare for the really risky situations.
Sometimes people face an unavoidable challenge that exceeds their comfort level. To help them prepare, create a series of activities with increasing similarity to the actual event.

Brian, a new sales manager who recently began working on his presentation skills, nearly panicked when his manager was called away on urgent business and he was thrust into a major customer presentation. Though he had practiced presentations in front of a mirror in the past, Linda, his coach, pointed out that talking to himself in the mirror bore little resemblance to fielding tough questions in a conference room.

Brian and Linda arranged three dry runs of the presentation, first in front of Linda and next with a small group of friendly peers. At the final dress rehearsal, an audience of Brian's colleagues was invited to raise issues and pose challenging questions. By the end of his third run-through, Brian's anxiety had dissipated and he was ready for the customer meeting.

This tactic of increasingly realistic trial runs works for other needs as well. People could ramp up their financial skills by preparing a preliminary budget analysis to compare with one created by someone with considerable experience. Next, they could prepare an analysis for actual submission, subject to expert review. Then, they might informally discuss their analysis with the management team. Finally, they might take full responsibility for the budget as implemented.

> **If you only do things you know well and do comfortably, you'll never reach higher goals.**
>
> *Linda Tsao Yang*

Break the Habit Cycle

The new behaviors people are trying to solidify usually have to compete with old, well-established habits. Unless the old is nudged out of the way, the new can't take hold. But habits often persist without conscious awareness, and opportunities for new behaviors often pass by unnoticed. To counterbalance these tendencies, people need to:
- Recognize their old habits so they can stop them.
- Anticipate what they will do differently in situations where old habits prevail.

Recognize old habits.

Interrupt habits on the fly. People can learn to identify cues that signal when they are slipping into old habits. Then, whenever they notice the signal, they can stop what they are doing and shift to their new skill instead of letting the old habit run its course.
- What are the *internal* emotional cues that an old habit might be clicking in? For example, does Carlos, who is trying to be a better listener, jump to conclusions and talk too much when he is feeling a lot of urgency to make a decision? Does he do this when he is frustrated or irritated? If so, whenever he feels impatient and irritated, he can remind himself to pause, ask questions, and paraphrase what other people are saying.
- What *external* cues signal an opportunity to apply the new skill? Do other people appear frustrated when Carlos doesn't listen? Do they remain quiet for long stretches of time? If so, whenever people appear frustrated or haven't said anything for a while in a conversation, he can be tipped off to switch from talking into listening mode.
- Enlist others to provide cues. Carlos had trouble noticing when he wasn't listening, but his staff didn't. So, he asked several people to alert him if they saw him talking too much.
- Plan a smooth transition. Once people interrupt their old habits, they should be prepared with a smooth transition into their new behavior. For example, each time Carlos catches himself, he stops talking and says, "Let me back up a second and get your input." Because this routine is so simple and natural, he doesn't stumble and look awkward while he shifts to listening.

Target trouble spots. Certain circumstances reliably trigger old habits. Even though she is trying to be more participative, Carolyn consistently takes over the agenda in staff meetings. Ray, who wants to contribute his technical expertise, finds that he defers to more senior engineers in design discussions. Carolyn and Ray are more likely to try their new skills if they gear up ahead of time for meetings where they are vulnerable to their old habits.
- The plan for development that you helped create in the *Inspire Commitment* strategy lists some of the triggers that prompt people to use their new skills. As people discover the situations that are most challenging, encourage them to incorporate new triggers into their plan. For example, Rhonda was trying to break the habit of making decisions solely on technical merit without considering market factors. As she planned her next project, she mapped out the junctures where she was likely to fall back on a quick technical solution instead of incorporating more market variables.
- Once the opportunities are identified, help people devise alternate actions to supplant the old habits. Rhonda's coach suggested she plan discussions with market-savvy colleagues prior to each project milestone, and enlist people to ask her, "How will the market respond to this?" each time an important decision is being finalized.

Challenge people to peak performance

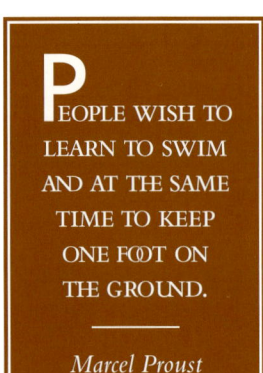

> People wish to learn to swim and at the same time to keep one foot on the ground.
>
> *Marcel Proust*

A personal athletic trainer sets high expectations and stretches people toward the limits of their potential with a regimen of practice, motivation, and goalsetting. In the same way, you can support, challenge, and push the bounds of people's capabilities. All the while, you walk the delicate line between pushing so hard that people become discouraged or easing up so much that they do not grow.

Foster continuous learning. The development journey is never complete, it just enters a new chapter.
- Encourage people to establish a continuous loop of feedback and information so they can adjust as circumstances change.
- Stir up fresh motivations by noting changing standards and emerging opportunities. Sustain the tension by highlighting the difference between where people are and where they want to be.
- Each person's optimal learning approach has its unique fingerprint. Encourage people to keep a log of their most successful learning experiences so they can institutionalize their best practices in their day-to-day activities.
- Cycle back to development needs that have not yet been pursued. Re-deploy the *Inspire Commitment* strategy around a new set of goals.

Let them go ahead of you. Since development is never complete, people need the freedom to make mistakes and need a continuous stream of encouragement, resources, and moral support. As their competencies grow, some of your students will surpass you. Keep them moving forward by:
- Helping them cultivate additional sources of support.
- Setting realistic expectations for your role so they do not become dependent on you for their development.
- Challenging your own willingness to allow people to excel. Pass tasks and opportunities to them that you have performed in the past. You may experience an urge to hold them back so you remain the expert. Resist that urge and rejoice in their ability to fly on their own.

Tips to help you promote persistence

- Remind people of their goals and their personal incentives.
- Reinforce people when they try something new or take intelligent risks.
- Sustain regular communication and updates on their development progress.
- Enlist others to acknowledge people's progress and encourage new approaches.
- Tell people to expect gradual increments in skill development.
- Help people identify old habits they need to break.
- Find opportunities where people can move their skill forward one step.
- Find two or three circumstances where their newly developed skill matches an organizational need.

In addition, the following tips might be useful for people in these coaching groups:

1. Set the standard.
- Set reasonable intermediate goals to prevent discouragement.
- Acknowledge incremental gains in skill; do not be afraid that people will stop working if they think they are making progress.
- Demonstrate your trust by giving them new tasks and autonomy.

2. Set new direction.
- Create opportunities for them to showcase their new skill with different types of people.
- Encourage them to discuss their challenges with colleagues who have similar goals or have gone through similar changes.
- Expose them to new information on the need for the skill, such as data on trends, articles by experts, and internal strategy documents.

3. Set free.
- Resist their tendency to spend time on skills and challenges they have already mastered.
- Push them to apply themselves under conditions of greater complexity, variety, difficulty, and stress.
- Continue to expose them to subject-area gurus inside and outside your organization.
- Guide them to opportunities to coach others, especially if you can link them with eager learners who may stretch and challenge their thinking.
- Free them from routine tasks where possible so they can devote more energy to specialized skills.
- Stimulate the need for them to perform at a higher level by providing a new assignment.
- Give them permission to cross-train in related areas and provide time to explore novel ideas.
- Create opportunities for them to benchmark their skills against experts.
- Show confidence in their potential to enter the realm of the elite.

Personal action steps

Master the basics: As you apply this strategy, make sure you have a solid foundation in:
- Providing credible, positive feedback.
- Encouraging others.

How will you encourage persistence in the person you are coaching?
- What is the person's greatest challenge as they apply their new skill? How will you help them overcome this challenge?
- Who needs someone with the skills that the person is developing? How can you be an advocate for their new skills?
- How will you help the person find opportunities to use the skills in new situations? How can you bring people into the situations that are under your direct control or influence?
- How will you help the person track their progress?
- What resources and support does the person need to continue using their new skills? How can you help provide these resources and support?
- How can you build their confidence and increase their willingness to take risks?

What have you learned so far about yourself as a coach?
- What insights do you want to remember from this chapter?
- What one or two things would make the most difference in your coaching?

Where will you begin to take action?
- What ideas are you going to try first?
- What will you incorporate into your plans for coaching others?
- What else do you need for your own development?

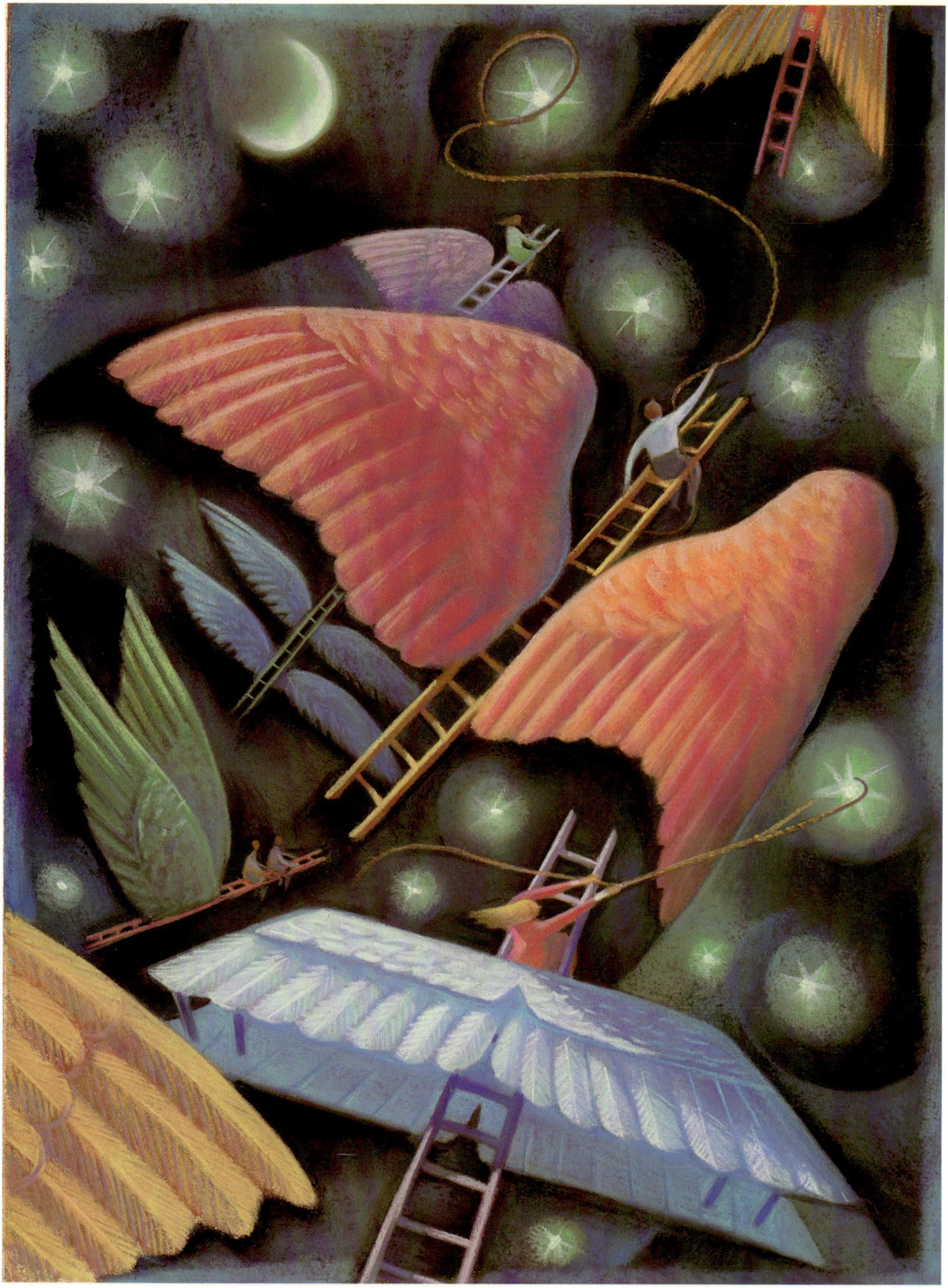

5. Shape the Environment

Build organizational support to reward learning and remove barriers.

Leader As Coach

Jump-start

Shaping the environment is most important when people:

- *Complain that management does not provide support or access to the right opportunities.*
- *Do not share their learning with others.*
- *Regard development as a distraction from their "real jobs."*
- *Express frustration at how difficult it is to develop.*
- *Claim that organizational rewards and incentives do not encourage development.*
- *Criticize management for just paying lip service to development.*

To shape the environment:

- *Publicly recognize and reward people who develop themselves and others.*
- *Demonstrate that you are personally engaged in development.*
- *Emphasize development in your department's business planning and performance management practices.*
- *Establish processes that promote learning from each other, both within and across departments.*
- *Influence the organization to include development measures in evaluations, reward systems, and climate surveys.*
- *Recruit senior managers for visible roles in development events.*

Strategy 5
SHAPE THE ENVIRONMENT

As people develop, the working environment can either propel them forward or obstruct their progress. People discern even subtle signals that telegraph whether they should forge ahead, retreat, or play it safe. To take the pulse on your development climate, consider these factors:
- Where can people see good role models for development?
- How is self-development valued and rewarded?
- What happens to people who risk trying new skills?
- How much do managers invest in developing their people?
- In what ways do organizational policies encourage people to invest in self-development?
- How often do people publicly talk about what they are learning?

Odds are, your environment sends mixed messages about the value of development. Even though you cannot completely control the environment's impact on people's development, there are many ways you can increase the odds that it is working for you, not against you. Your primary tactics are to:
- **Build your visibility as a role model.** Set an example through how you act and what you do to develop yourself.
- **Strengthen the learning climate in your area.** Make development a priority for your team through your attention and rewards.
- **Leverage organizational culture and systems.** Use existing systems to promote learning. Be an advocate for systems and policies that are conducive to development.

The payoffs for your efforts will be faster, more lasting change. No longer will people be able to claim that they would change but for the obstacles thrown in their path. And your entire team will build the cohesion and support that generates real enthusiasm for mutual learning.

> **CAPSULE PREVIEW**
>
> – *Diagnose organizational obstacles to development.*
>
> – *Walk your talk by developing yourself.*
>
> – *Create a local learning climate.*
>
> – *Influence your organization's culture and systems.*

Diagnose organizational obstacles to development

Coaches sometimes ignore legitimate organizational obstacles to development. To make sure you don't do this, look for the grain of truth in people's protests – even when they complain or blame others – so you can identify obstacles in the system or the source of the complaints. Find out if others agree on the problem.

The following comments from a survey of development practices across a range of organizations indicate potential organizational obstacles to development.[12] As you read the rest of the chapter, identify ideas you can use to prevent such concerns from being easy excuses.

I don't have enough time.
- There's no time to spend on development; just doing my job takes more hours than I have.
- It's not a priority in light of everything else we need to do.
- In a high-growth company, there's too much emphasis on results and profits to spend time on long-term development issues.

Leaders don't support development.
- Management just pays lip service.
- HR provides an infrastructure, but the corporate group doesn't provide support at the top.
- There is never any real money in the budget for development.
- People at corporate HR believe very strongly in coaching, but it doesn't filter down to the business units, because senior management doesn't walk the talk.

Development won't make a difference.
- All they care about is if I make my numbers, so why spend my time on something that doesn't matter.
- It's just another flavor of the month.
- Everything in our business changes too fast anyway.
- It's not part of my goals.
- The people who develop themselves don't get promoted; it still depends on who you know.

Walk your talk by developing yourself

Whether you like it or not, you are already a role model. The people you lead listen to what you say, watch what you do, and compare your words with your actions to gauge your consistency.

If your entreaties for people to develop are backed with investment in your own growth, people are more likely to believe that you mean business. Unfortunately, many managers believe that it is more important to develop others than to develop themselves.[13] If you are among them, and you aren't setting a good example, you might be jettisoning your best chance to convince people that development really matters.

Start by being coachable yourself, and then making your self-development visible. While you should pursue coaching from many sources, you set a powerful example if you are open to learning from the people you coach. Then, you not only model openness to development, you also strengthen the trust that is so vital to a strong coaching partnership.

When Jan, an IT manager in a computer and technology organization, didn't get the promotion she expected, she was puzzled and disappointed. After a rapid rise, her career trajectory had flattened out. When she asked around to find out why she had stalled, she discovered that she was viewed as a tactician who was well regarded by the engineers, but who lacked the leadership fortitude and perspective to run a business unit. Recognizing more than a grain of truth in these perceptions, Jan resolved to change.

She began by recruiting her team as active allies in her development. She talked openly with them about her goals. "When I look at myself and where our company is headed, I think I need to be more strategic. I also need to be more willing to make tough decisions. I've asked for help from Patrick in marketing, because he has such a broad

> CEOs can be more powerful role models, when they learn rather than when they teach.
>
> *Rosabeth Moss Kanter*

If you want to be a coach, be coachable.

view of our business. And, I'd like you to let me know when you think I should let go of everyday tasks and take a longer view."

She also explained her intention to follow her own advice. "I've been encouraging you to take more risks. Now it's time for me to take some risks, too. It's going to be hard for me to be more decisive because I tend to look for consensus. But I want you to push me to take a stand."

Finally, Jan let her team know that she doesn't want to be blindsided again. "I was surprised by the feedback about my style. I guess I lost touch when my role and the business shifted in the past couple of years. I don't want that to happen again, so I'm asking all of you to be honest with me about what I need to do differently. I'd rather have you be blunt than keep your thoughts to yourselves."

Like Jan, here are some ways you can be an effective role model:

Make your self-development visible. To demonstrate vividly that C&D matters, let people see you develop. Through your actions and words, you can make every step of your development visible, including choosing priorities, pushing your comfort zone, reflecting on progress, and seeking information and feedback. Highlight development in your daily activities and choices:
- "I'd like to be involved in the financial planning for that project so I can keep working on my financial skills."
- "During our meeting today, catch me when I go off on tangents. Flag me so I can get back on track."
- "I've been reflecting on my presentation at the customer meeting yesterday. I spent too much time going over our new features. I still need to work on speaking directly to customer needs."

Showcase your improvements. Let people know the tangible outcomes of your development by contrasting your old skills with the new.
- "Before I worked on my conflict management skills, I was stumped when people challenged me directly. But last week when Terry started arguing with me in the staff meeting, I listened instead of automatically fighting back."
- "Lately, I've had much more appreciation for the different ways that people look at things, so I've tried to cut down on giving advice. Instead, I try to get people to think things through themselves. They come up with things I never thought of."
- "I've tried to take on more assignments that give me a chance to work on my writing. I think it's paying off. Our department head asked me to draft a public relations piece for our new system."

Pave the way for better feedback. Just like the people you are coaching, you won't know how you are doing without good information from others. Your open-door policy and requests for candor alone will rarely open the feedback floodgates. You can help information flow your way if you make it easy for others to talk with you about how you are doing.
- At key junctures, such as after a meeting or a tough decision, ask for feedback about how you handled the situation.
- Make two-way feedback discussions a habit. At the end of each chat about other people's development, ask them how they see you and what you could do to be more effective.
- Create safe ways for people to give you feedback. Ask your HR person to check on people's perceptions of your progress or use a standardized confidential feedback survey.
- Include feedback on your development progress in reviews of your performance and projects. Invite your supervisor to talk with people who work with you to get their perspective on your skills and your progress.

> WHEN THE MASTER MAKES A MISTAKE, SHE REALIZES IT. HAVING REALIZED IT, SHE ADMITS IT. HAVING ADMITTED IT, SHE CORRECTS IT. SHE CONSIDERS THOSE WHO POINT OUT THE FAULTS AS HER MOST BENEVOLENT TEACHERS.
>
> *Tao Te Ching*

Create a local learning climate

People's development journeys are challenging enough without the added burden of hacking through the underbrush of competing agendas, scarce development resources, and paltry rewards that suggest it's not worth the effort. As a coach, you can clear a path for people through this jungle.

Start by simply letting people know that you value learning and intend to make it a priority. Then, back your words with the resources and opportunities you directly influence, including:
- Budgets.
- Team and individual goals.
- Meeting agendas.
- Group communications.
- Assignments.
- Staffing decisions.
- Compensation and other rewards.
- Celebrations.
- Performance evaluations.

Leveraging these resources and opportunities, you can highlight the importance of continuous development with the following:
- Make it safer to go out on a limb by encouraging people to try new things and by dealing constructively with their failures.
- Make everyone a learner and everyone a teacher so people readily learn from each other.
- Align your existing management processes with development, so everyday activities reinforce development action.

> Do what you can, with what you have, where you are.
>
> *Theodore Roosevelt*

Make it safer to go out on a limb

Perhaps your most difficult challenge in creating a learning climate is sustaining people's willingness to take risks. Permeate your work context with the message that trying new things is not only allowed, but expected.

Support well-calculated experimentation so people have the opportunity to test the boundaries of what they are capable of doing.
- Demonstrate that you are willing to let people tackle new responsibilities while they are still learning. The next time someone says, "What would happen if..." encourage them to try it and find out. When you authorize people to do things for which they might not believe they are ready, you imbue them with your confidence in their ability.
- Catch yourself when you are tempted to give assignments to the resident expert instead of the apprentice. People will be more willing to test their wings if they know that others are being pushed out of the nest also.
- Publicly accept the mistakes that are inevitable when people are learning. Don't let others sound the alarm when mistakes happen, either. Let people know that you expect – and even desire – mistakes as evidence that they are trying and learning new things.
- Discuss mistakes openly, instead of downplaying or ignoring them, so everyone can learn from the example. Point out your own mistakes and what you have learned from them.

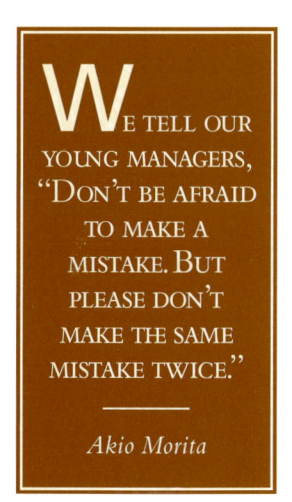

> We tell our young managers, "Don't be afraid to make a mistake. But please don't make the same mistake twice."
>
> *Akio Morita*

> MISHAPS ARE LIKE KNIVES, THAT EITHER SERVE US OR CUT US, AS WE GRASP THEM BY THE BLADE OR THE HANDLE.
>
> *Herman Melville*

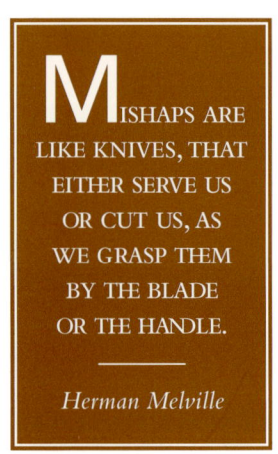

Tolerate isolated failures. After years of fruitless trial and error, Thomas Edison was closing in on the discovery of the proper filament for the electric light bulb. Producing each new filament and test bulb required hours of intense effort. Moments before a crucial test, Edison and his colleagues watched as a young worker, carrying the latest bulb, tripped on the stairs and shattered the bulb on the floor. The air was thick with the disappointment of the entire team. The next day, after another concentrated effort, Edison showed his willingness to tolerate mistakes by asking that same young worker to carry the new bulb to the test site. That spirit was a crucial ingredient in Edison's genius for innovation.

Foster a shared sense of purpose. A shared vision helps people escape the gravitational force field of the status quo. People with a powerful sense of purpose are more eager to learn and more willing to experiment with new behaviors. Robert Haas, CEO at Levi Strauss, says their vision and values statement "allows individuals to take risks that they couldn't take if they weren't bound together by a common understanding."[14] It also keeps people focused on the skills that are most important for the long haul.

Make everyone a learner and everyone a teacher

You may need to shatter some expectations that team performance and individual expertise are immune from critique. In a learning climate, people can't pretend that they know everything. Confidence and pride in their expertise are useful when trying new things. But these same qualities can interfere with the humility needed for people to listen to each other, share their observations and reactions, and ask for as well as offer help. Instead of protecting their stature, people need to crave what they can learn from each other and be willing to share what they know.

Aim to create a climate where candor about shortcomings is a virtue and openness about problems is a route to greater achievement.

Cut through taboos about group interaction. Mutual learning is impeded when a group doesn't openly face its own challenges. You can prod everyone to come clean with their opinions and experiences when you make group process and team dynamics open subjects for feedback and constructive criticism.
- When a discussion hits a roadblock, take a moment to acknowledge it, explore the cause, and propose alternate ways of proceeding.
- Spend two or three minutes at the end of each meeting evaluating what worked well, so you solidify your understanding of what maintains a positive environment. Similarly, bring to the surface what is not working well and solicit suggestions about what the group could do differently to improve subsequent meetings.
- Periodically ask people how comfortable they feel speaking their minds. Establish group ground rules that promote candor and then vigilantly enforce them.

> The job of senior management... is to create an environment where [store managers] can learn from the market — and from each other.
>
> Sam Walton

Encourage constructive conflict. When people dance around their personal differences, it's hard for them to build the trust required for mutual learning.
- Make sure that conflict remains positive by keeping the focus on the problem, not on the people.
- When you sense that only one view of a situation has been raised, ask pointedly for other opinions. Listen attentively when people voice contrary views. Ask enough questions to make sure others feel heard in full.
- Designate someone to play the devil's advocate role in group discussions.
- When defensiveness arises, seek to understand its cause, because defensiveness often signals that something important is not being discussed.

Ease up on the decision-making throttle. For people to develop, they need new ideas and perspectives. The unceasing urgency to make decisions, however, tends to drive people to follow the same old routes to the same old conclusions. You open new opportunities for learning when you intercept this automatic surge and rechannel it toward less well-worn paths.
- Because new ideas often take time to percolate, protect novel suggestions and make room for creativity. Redirect people's attention to make sure they fully consider alternatives that are reflexively overlooked.
- Monitor the speed of decision making on issues where new learning is pertinent. Specifically ask people to apply their new ideas and skills to the problem. Ask the group if the issue has been explored in sufficient depth, taking particular pains to tap the views of the more quiet members. Wait until adequate exploration and divergence of thinking have occurred before allowing decisions. This does not mean that you delay conclusions unnecessarily, but that you make a conscious decision to ensure that new learning and ideas have been tapped.

> THERE IS NO WISDOM LIKE FRANKNESS.
>
> *Benjamin Disraeli*

Encourage dialog about "how" as well as "what." People learn more from hearing the inside story than from seeing a glossy picture of the final results.
- Use updates to do more than simply report what people did or didn't accomplish. Instead, ask people to describe new things they tried, what they struggled with, and how they responded.
- Invite people to share with other team members what they have learned recently. Facilitate discussion of how the lesson can be applied in other situations and by other people.
- Create a forum where the group can critique each other's successes and failures to dissect what worked and what didn't. Project milestones, quarterly planning sessions, and customer reviews are among the natural junctures for reflection on group learning. To reinforce the value of experimentation, look for the upside of failures and the room for improvement in successes. Guide people to extract the lessons that can be applied to other circumstances.

Dave Marsing, manager of Intel's largest semiconductor plant, regularly asks people to examine what is really going on.

After important meetings, for example, Marsing has been known to send out a common memo to every attendee asking not the typical questions ("How did it go?" or "What decision did the group reach?"), but something entirely unexpected, such as "Explain the dynamics of the meeting." Such a question forces the participants not merely to parrot the end result but actually to consider how they got there.

"I want people to think about how they got to a decision," Marsing says, "because in the long run, their understanding of the process, of how they related to one another, is more important than a single result."[15]

Highlight C&D heroes. Visibly reward people who:
- Consistently work on their own development by learning from others.
- Make mistakes, learn from them, and share their insights with others.
- Develop in ways that contribute to shared objectives.
- Invest in coaching and developing others.

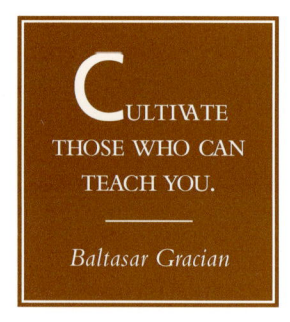

> Cultivate those who can teach you.
>
> *Baltasar Gracian*

Align your existing management practices with development

You probably make decisions every week that influence whether the people around you take coaching and development seriously. These might be conscious decisions that force you to sacrifice one priority for another, or inadvertently missed opportunities for promoting your coaching and development agenda.

As you consider how well your decisions align with C&D, review the following scenarios in which four managers took different approaches to reshape their management practices. Look also for other openings for greater alignment, such as department mission statements and decisions about pay and bonuses.

Budgeting and goal setting. The vice president of sales at a financial services firm describes how she aligned her annual budgeting process:

Last year, one of my managers asked me why our division never spent its budget for leadership development even though we overspent our technical training budget. That question really got me to think. I'd always thought I was supporting development by having such a clear line item in my budget. But what was the point if people didn't use it? So when we began budgeting for this year, I asked each department manager to include aggressive performance targets for improving the quality of leadership. That startled a few people, but it led to some good conversations with people about how important it is to develop our leadership talent.

Performance reviews. A regional manager in a prestigious consulting firm took the following action:

Our whole performance evaluation process has been pretty loose. One of our managers constantly complained that performance reviews were a waste of time: "Every year I just hear the same old things." Finally, his boss cut through his gripes with razor clarity: "Then why haven't you done anything about it?" That story put me over the edge on the importance of actually working on development. I ended up working with HR to add four development categories to our performance reviews:
• What are their career goals and development priorities?
• What is their plan for working on their priorities?
• How will they get feedback to measure their progress?
• What organizational support and resources do they need?
Then, to put some teeth into it, we made self-development account for 10-20% of their evaluation, depending on their other priorities.

Weekly staff meetings. This manufacturing manager realized that he could easily reinforce the importance of development in his team meetings:

I have always kept my staff meetings very focused, so people usually came prepared to talk about three topics: problems to solve, information to share, and milestones to recognize. I realized one day that we only talked about business issues. We never talked about people's challenges as coaches or what they were learning. So I added a fourth topic to our agenda to make sure development was on the scope. It took a while to get going, but every week one or two people have something to report. I summarize what they've done in my monthly report as well.

Staffing decisions. The rapid pace of change in the high-tech industry led this research and development manager to change how he hires and promotes people:

> Determine if job candidates will continue to learn.

Until recently, I hired people strictly based on their ability to do the job. Now, when making staff decisions, I try to determine how well they will continue to learn on the job. We factor development into promotions, too, by hiring people who have a good track record of learning and self-improvement. Technical skills are still important, but we've changed the job interview to include questions like:
- What are the three most important lessons you've learned in your career? How did you learn them?
- What have you done to develop yourself in the last year?
- How did you respond the last time you made a major mistake?
- How did you respond the last time someone on your team made a major mistake?
- What have you done to help others develop? Who have you helped?

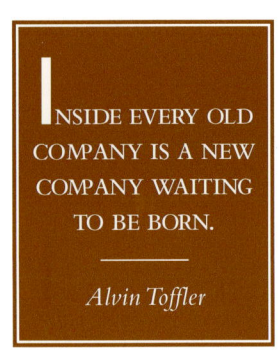

> **I**NSIDE EVERY OLD COMPANY IS A NEW COMPANY WAITING TO BE BORN.
>
> *Alvin Toffler*

Influence your organization's culture and systems.

If leaders' attitudes and practices are at odds with C&D, they assert considerable drag on people's energy and motivation to develop. Listen in on these observations from senior managers:[16]

- Our reward system has historically reinforced a 'lone ranger' mentality. People aren't incented to provide or promote coaching.
- People are reluctant to provide coaching to minorities or older workers for fear of EEO or age discrimination impact. They're afraid people will say, "I was told to develop this skill and then I still didn't get the job."
- Coaching is not part of the culture. People don't feel comfortable doing coaching. The organization is very results-oriented and they don't tell you what to do to change, only that you need to change.
- People here say, "What's the use of taking the time when senior managers won't do it? I'll just concentrate on making my numbers."
- We have two cultures: The old autocrats reject coaching and any participative management practice, while giving it lip service. But results talk in this culture, and if people produce, they're allowed to continue the old management style.

If these complaints sound familiar, you and your people might be fighting an uphill battle on the development front. While some of the variables that sustain such systemic barriers are outside your control, you would be remiss as a coach if you failed to do what you could to push back at organizational policies, procedures, and processes when you *can* make a difference.

While you don't need to be a crusader for a major culture change, if you challenge, inform, and tweak the culture at those points where it intersects with what you are doing, you help it work for you instead of against you. Directly and indirectly, you prod other leaders to think in new ways and you keep development on the organization's agenda. And, you also show the people you coach the depth of your commitment to development.

Do your leaders walk the talk or do they stumble the mumble?

IT IS BETTER TO LIGHT ONE CANDLE THAN CURSE THE DARKNESS.

Motto of the Christopher Society

Think globally, act locally

By thinking globally and acting locally, you can advocate a climate conducive to development. In this example, Antonio, a department manager, pursues his C&D agenda in a conversation with Lisa, the general manager:

"Lisa, I'm running into a wall here. I haven't found anyone in senior management who really believes we need to invest in developing people. They keep talking about long-term competitiveness, but then they just look at short-term results. They can't have it both ways."

"Well, Antonio, what do you think we should be doing?"

"Lots of things. They could allocate more time and money for training and professional conferences. They could tell us how we're doing. The only feedback we ever get is 'Nice work. See if you can increase profitability a bit more.' I wonder if you could do anything to help."

Lisa pushed back. "I'd love to, but let's look at some things you could do also."

"I could route that article I sent you about gaining competitive advantage through learning. I've also been thinking about pounding out a memo on our lack of rewards and incentives for coaching and development. Unless they put their money where their mouth is, nothing will change."

"I suspect lots of people agree with you. Have you thought about who else might be willing to help?"

After a moment's contemplation, Antonio responded. "Obviously I could talk with HR. And I could touch base with Todd over in operations. He has a pretty good reputation for developing folks. He might be able to say a few things in management committee meetings."

"With all the changes going on around here, I know staff development isn't necessarily on the radar screen for a lot of senior managers. You're going to need to think about how you can get their attention," cautioned Lisa.

"I'm sure they'll want data on whether it will be worth the cost. There has to be some research on the topic. Maybe HR could help track it down. It would be great if we could conduct a small experiment – pilot something – to see what the payback for more development would be."

Antonio demonstrated several tactics that almost anyone can use to influence their organizational culture and systems:

Communicate. Begin to make some noise, because concerns and frustrations often don't filter upward to the policy makers, and even when they do they may not be recognized as crucial. The old adage "The squeaky wheel gets the grease" contains a large kernel of truth. Look for ways to capture people's attention by repeating your message in different ways.

Educate. Spread the word on the benefits of learning and development. Draw on books such as *The Tom Peters Seminar* or *The Learning Edge*[17] that illustrate the link between C&D and organizational strategy.

Make it easy for people to gain access to knowledge and tools for putting development into practice, such as the book *Development FIRST*. Sponsor a quarterly forum with internal and external experts on the topic of development. Compare development practices in your organization with the best practices followed by organizations that have reputations for development excellence.

Affiliate. Cultivate relationships with the informal playmakers and people in power. They can sponsor and model good development practices.

Illustrate. When you create tangible evidence that development works, you cut through skepticism and create a strong bargaining chip. Start with a small project where approval is relatively easy, designing it to trip the hot buttons that ignite organizational momentum. Antonio, for example, knew that his culture valued facts, particularly if they were connected to tangible results. He knew that pleas not backed with proof were likely to be ignored. With a successful pilot run, he could bolster his chance to influence larger changes.

Adapt Processes to Drive Change

Lily, a marketing manager in a fast-paced technology company, transferred into a traditional product group with the mandate to make it more agile and competitive. She quickly recognized that continuous learning was crucial to her success and that few existing organizational initiatives reinforced a development culture. While Antonio, in the previous example, opted for a direct advocacy approach to influence his organization, Lily decided to adapt existing practices to support her development priorities. Notice how she redefined processes to stretch her people and how she required management to support development as well.

At first I thought I had the support of senior management, but I soon realized they wanted me to make the changes so they didn't have to rock the boat themselves. The people I had to influence the most were higher than me in the organization. It wasn't hard to figure out that if I made too many waves, I wouldn't be around long myself.

So I looked for existing processes that I could leverage to start to shape change. I chose three things that were a strong part of the current culture.

First, we conduct an annual organizational survey that evaluates management practices, morale, and work climate. Of course, there was nothing in the survey on innovation or learning. But it had a section that allowed new items every year. I made sure it included several questions about risk taking, getting honest performance feedback, management support for learning, development resources, etc. I hoped that once it was measured, people would start to do something about it. And I could always use that data to support other changes I thought were needed.

Second, senior management tracked a number of business and process measures such as time-to-market and customer complaint resolution.

> Nothing great is created suddenly, any more than a bunch of grapes or a fig. Let it first blossom, then bear fruit, then ripen.
>
> *Epictetus*

I displayed that information prominently and started raising the targets. Then I met with the team to talk about how we could change and what we needed from senior management to achieve those goals. I always tried to show how development needs tied in directly to customer needs. Then, in return for support, I let senior management take credit for our improvements. When they saw what we were doing, they began to look for ways to roll out what we had learned in other areas.

Third, it was common to hold small, informal celebrations when the team accomplished key milestones. I started holding similar celebrations to recognize learning-related activities, such as trying new things, taking reasonable risks, and working on self-development activities. Most importantly, I invited different senior managers to speak and be a part of these celebrations. Although they might have felt somewhat coerced into coming, the whole team thanked them and the senior managers started to get the flavor and excitement of the new learning environment.

Although the specifics will differ in your situation, at least two principles from Lily's work should apply to your change initiatives:

Reshape existing systems and processes. Rather than trying to create new measures, Lily piggybacked on tools that people already used.

Leverage senior management involvement. Lily featured senior management in several of her actions and gave them credit. That goodwill paved the way for further support. In addition, their involvement helped to change their attitudes about the value of development.

Tips to help you shape the environment

- Ask a colleague or someone from Human Resources to help you audit how well your management practices support development.
- Ask people what additional organizational support they would like.
- Form a coalition of those who share your focus on C&D to influence organizational policies and practices.
- Ask a peer, a direct report, and a higher level manager for feedback on your personal development and the visibility and effectiveness of your development of others.
- Look for one opportunity a day to talk with someone new about the importance of development.
- Read works by Chris Argyris, such as the article "Teaching smart people how to learn," where he outlines techniques to increase learning through dialog and exploration.
- Read one of these books on learning in organizations: Kline and Saunders' *Ten Steps to a Learning Organization,* Marquardt and Reynolds' *The Global Learning Organization,* Senge's *The Fifth Discipline*, or Wick and Leon's *The Learning Edge.*

In addition, the following tips might be useful for people in these coaching groups:

1. Set the standard.
- Let others know that you have given new opportunities to people who are still learning.
- Challenge any organizational tendencies to look the other way when people underperform.
- Scrutinize existing feedback and performance evaluation processes to make sure they support candid discussion of people's performance against standards.

2. Set new direction.
- Set a goal that everyone you coach will learn something in a completely new area this year.
- Break down organizational barriers that limit people's opportunities to try new things.
- Set consistent goals for everyone on the team to change in ways that support your area's strategic focus.
- Demonstrate what you are personally doing to adapt to organizational and competitive changes.

3. Set free.
- Challenge people who make budget decisions to allocate resources for cultivating cutting-edge expertise.
- Influence priorities and rewards to reinforce experimental application of expertise to new areas.
- Demonstrate that you seek mentoring and feedback from others, even in areas where your skills are already solid.

Personal action steps

Master the basics. As you apply this strategy, make sure you have a solid foundation in:
- Self-development.
- Seeking feedback.
- Influencing and networking.
- Political savvy and organizational astuteness.

How will you apply this strategy to your environment?
- What are the development barriers that people mention most frequently? How can you have an impact to remove those barriers?
- Which of your management practices are out of sync with C&D? How can you change them?
- What can you do to be a more effective role model for self-development?
- What organizational practices seem most important for you to try to influence? What strategies can you use?
- What are the catalysts for development in your environment and how can you use them to your advantage? Who can be your allies in change?

What have you learned about yourself as a coach?
- What insights do you want to remember from this chapter?
- What one or two things would make the most difference in your coaching?

Where will you begin to take action?
- What ideas are you going to try first?
- What will you incorporate into your plans for coaching others?
- What else do you need for your own development?

References

Argyris, C. (1991). Teaching smart people how to learn. *Harvard Business Review,* May-June, 99-109.

Covey, S. (1989). *Seven Habits of Highly Effective People.* New York: Simon & Schuster.

Davis, B. L., Skube, C. J., Hellervik, L. W., Gebelein, S. H., & Sheard, J. L. (1996). *Successful Manager's Handbook.* Minneapolis: Personnel Decisions International.

Ferguson, M. (1980). *The Aquarian Conspiracy: Personal and Social Transformation in the 1980s.* Los Angeles: J. P. Tarcher.

Gaugler, B. B., Rosenthal, D. B., Thornton, G. C., & Bentson, C. (1987). Meta-analysis of assessment center validity. *Journal of Applied Psychology,* 72, 493-511.

Grabow, K. M. (1989). The roles of developmental events and individual differences in managerial success. Unpublished doctoral dissertation. Minneapolis: University of Minnesota.

Heine, D. M., & Peterson, D. B. (1994). The quest for competitive advantage: Aligning organizational and individual change. Executive forum, Personnel Decisions, Inc.

Kline, P., & Saunders, B. (1993). *Ten Steps to a Learning Organization.* Arlington, VA: Great Ocean Publishers.

Malone, M. S. (1995). Killer results without killing yourself. *Fast Company,* 1(1), 125-132.

Marquardt, M., & Reynolds, A. (1994). *The Global Learning Organization.* Burr Ridge, IL: Irwin.

Mitchell, R., & Oneal, M. (1994). Managing by values. *Business Week,* August 1, 46-52.

Peters, T. (1994). *The Tom Peters Seminar: Crazy Times Call for Crazy Organizations.* New York: Vintage.

Peterson, D. B., & Hicks, M. D. (1995). *Development FIRST: Strategies for Self-Development.* Minneapolis: Personnel Decisions International.

Peterson, D. B., Uranowitz, S. W., & Hicks, M. D. (1996). Management coaching at work: Survey of current practices in Fortune 250 organizations. Paper presented at the annual conference of the American Psychological Association, Toronto.

Peterson, D. B., Uranowitz, S. W., & Ronnkvist, A. R. (1995). Personal development: It's important for you but not for me. Unpublished research, Personnel Decisions International.

Ramstad, P. M. (1995, October). Measuring and improving human assets with a financial asset management model. Presentation at the International Assessment Conference, Dallas. Personnel Decisions International and Texas Instruments.

Senge, P. M. (1990). *The Fifth Discipline: The Art and Practice of the Learning Organization.* New York: Doubleday/Currency.

Tully, S. (1995). So, Mr. Bossidy, we know that you can cut. Now show us how to grow. *Fortune,* August 21, 70-80.

Wick, C. W., & Leon, L. S. (1993). *The Learning Edge.* New York: McGraw-Hill.

Notes

1. Ramstad (1995).

2. Ferguson (1980).

3. Peterson, Uranowitz, & Hicks (1996).

4. Peterson, Uranowitz, & Hicks (1996).

5. Covey (1989).

6. Peterson, Uranowitz, & Hicks (1996).

7. Covey (1989).

8. Grabow (1989), p. 139.

9. An alternative powerful way to prepare people for future organizational changes is to use simulations or development centers that replicate various challenging business scenarios. See Gaugler (1987) or Heine & Peterson (1994).

10. Davis et al. (1996).

11. Tully (1995), p. 73.

12. Peterson, Uranowitz, & Hicks (1996).

13. Peterson, Uranowitz, & Ronnkvist (1995).

14. Mitchell and Oneal (1994), p. 49.

15. Malone (1995), p. 30.

16. Peterson, Uranowitz, & Hicks (1996).

17. Peters (1995); Wick & Leon (1993).

Biographies

Mary Dee Hicks and **David Peterson,** Senior Vice Presidents at Personnel Decisions International, have devoted much of their careers to helping organizations and their people become stronger through the development of individual talents. Their consulting experience spans dozens of prominent international organizations, including *Fortune* 100 firms such as Hewlett-Packard, 3M, Ford, and PepsiCo.

As psychologists and leadership coaches, they have cultivated practical approaches to development that have been consolidated into workshops, presentations, and publications, including *Development FIRST: Strategies for Self-Development* and *Leader As Coach: Strategies for Coaching and Developing Others.*

To order copies of *Development FIRST, Leader As Coach, Successful Manager's Handbook,* or *The Executive Handbook,* or to obtain more information about PDI, mail the attached card or call your local office. In the U.S. call 1.800.633.4410.

Successful Manager's Handbook—Over 700,000 copies in print. This 800-page reference book provides practical tips, on-the-job activities, and suggestions for improving managerial skills and effectiveness.

Development FIRST—This easy-to-read book walks people through proven, practical steps to development. It helps them assess what they should work on, pick the right approaches and tactics, and learn from their experiences.

The Executive Handbook is the result of years of work with many successful *Fortune* 500 executives who lead today's high performance organizations. It is based on the same competency model as PDI's Executive Success Profile, which identifies the eight factors essential to executive success in every industry.

OUTSIDE THE USA

☐ Please send me _____ copies of *Leader As Coach.*
☐ Please send me _____ copies of *Development FIRST.*
☐ Please send me _____ copies of *Successful Manager's Handbook.*
☐ Please send me _____ copies of *The Executive Handbook.*
☐ Please send me information on other publications from Personnel Decisions International.
☐ Please send me information on consulting, products, and services from Personnel Decisions International.

Name_____
Title_____
Organization_____
Address_____
_____
City_____
Postal Code_____Country_____
Telephone_____

Charge to: ☐ VISA ☐ MC ☐ AMEX
Card Number_____
Exp. Date_____
Signature_____
Please allow 2-3 weeks for delivery

Mail or FAX this form to (001)612.904.7120.   COACH 499

US REPLY CARD

☐ Please send me _____ copies of *Leader As Coach.* $19.95 U.S. per book, plus shipping & handling.
☐ Please send me _____ copies of *Development FIRST.* $16.95 U.S. per book, plus shipping & handling.
☐ Please send me _____ copies of *Successful Manager's Handbook.* $54.95 U.S. per book, plus shipping & handling.
☐ Please send me _____ copies of *The Executive Handbook.* $75.00 U.S. per book, plus shipping & handling.
☐ Please send me information on other publications from Personnel Decisions International.
☐ Please send me information on consulting, products, and services from Personnel Decisions International.

Name_____
Title_____
Organization_____
Address_____
_____
City_____
State_____Zip Code_____
Telephone_____

Charge to: ☐ VISA ☐ MC ☐ AMEX
Card Number_____
Exp. Date_____
Signature_____
Please allow 2-3 weeks for delivery

Mail or FAX this form to 612.904.7120, or call 800.633.4410.   COACH 499

POSTAGE
HERE

PERSONNEL DECISIONS INTERNATIONAL
PEAVEY7-TJ
2000 PLAZA VII TOWER
45 SOUTH SEVENTH STREET
MINNEAPOLIS, MN 55402-1608
USA

BUSINESS REPLY MAIL
FIRST-CLASS PERMIT NO. 13372 MINNEAPOLIS, MN

POSTAGE WILL BE PAID BY THE ADDRESSEE
PERSONNEL DECISIONS INTERNATIONAL
PEAVEY7-TJ
2000 PLAZA VII TOWER
45 SOUTH SEVENTH STREET
MINNEAPOLIS, MN 55402-9891

NO POSTAGE
NECESSARY
IF MAILED
IN THE
UNITED STATES